Skijor With Your Dog

Skijor With Your Dog

Mari Høe-Raitto

and

Carol Kaynor

University of Alaska Press
Fairbanks

Published by
University of Alaska Press
P.O. Box 756240
Fairbanks, AK 99775-6240

ISBN 978-1-60223-186-3 (paperback); 978-1-60223-187-0 (electronic)

First edition © 1991 Mari Høe-Raitto and Carol Kaynor, published by OK
Publishing

Library of Congress Cataloging-in-Publication Data

Høe-Raitto, Mari, 1959–
Skijor with your dog / by Mari Høe-Raitto & Carol Kaynor.—2nd ed.
      p. cm.
Mari Høe-Raitto listed first on prev. ed.
Includes bibliographical references and index.
      ISBN 978-1-60223-186-3 (alk. paper)—ISBN 978-1-60223-187-0
      1. Skijoring with dogs. I. Kaynor, Carol, 1955– II. Høe-Raitto, Mari,
1959– Skijor with your dog. III. Title.
GV857.S48H54 2012
796.93—dc23
                              2012005519

Cover design by 5th Avenue Graphics
Cover illustration: Sara Elzey and Avril. Photo by Dave Partee.
Interior design and layout by Paula Elmes

This publication was printed on acid-free paper that meets the minimum
requirements for ANSI / NISO Z39.48–1992 (R2002) (Permanence of Paper
for Printed Library Materials).

Contents

To my father, Ole Jakob Høe, who taught me the love of animals and gave me the inspiration to believe in myself and make my dream possible.

To my mom, Gerd Østensvig Høe, who taught me understanding, patience, and love for people and animals.

To Leo, Sam, Camille, and all my other dogs over the years that made me who I am as a dog person.

—M.H.R.

To little Willow—my second Willow—who is teaching me how much I still don't know about dogs; to Lynn, who gave her to me; and to all the other wonderful, "imperfect" dogs, past and present, who have graced my life.

—C.K.

Acknowledgments for the Second Edition

Many people helped us put together this edition of the book. Fred Raymond of Raven Cross Country improved the section on ski equipment and loaned us skis, boots, and poles for a photo shoot. Chuck and Tone Deehr provided information on Jeff Conn's plans for insulated doghouses. Hege Ingebrigtsen, Amy Cooper, and Lena Boysen Hillestad provided dryland information. Helen Lundberg and Greg Sellentin helped locate photos.

We are grateful to all the authors whose reference lists helped us update our bibliography and add new books of note. In particular, Miki and Julie Collins's excellent book, *Dog Driver: A Guide for the Serious Musher*, has a comprehensive and extremely useful resource section.

Several photographers contributed photos to this new edition, for which we are deeply grateful. Andrea Swingley helped with photo selection and offered tips on organizing and processing. Marge Thompson of Digital Photographic Services at the UAF Rasmuson Library scanned artwork from the first edition, and Charles Mason of the UAF Department of Journalism helped with photographs from the first edition. Dave Partee provided many of the photos in this edition and spent countless hours on image processing. Sara Elzey graciously participated in multiple photo shoots for the cover image.

Encouragement and moral support, and in some cases food, were provided by several people, especially Hilary Alejandro, Vladimir Borschev, Mark Douglas, Barbara Partee, Dave Partee, Amy Simpson, and Andrea Swingley.

A complete draft of the text for the second edition was due to our new publisher, University of Alaska Press, at an extremely busy time for Carol. She could not possibly have met that deadline without the help of Barbara Partee and Vladimir Borschev.

If we have forgotten to acknowledge anyone who helped us, we sincerely apologize. Thank you to all, named and unnamed, for your support and assistance.

Thanks go to Laura Walker, James Engelhardt, and Sue Mitchell at University of Alaska Press for their time, attention, encouragement, and, in Sue's case, patience with an author who knew enough to be dangerous but not enough to realize she'd bitten off more than she could chew.

A very special thank-you goes to our champion, Amy Simpson of University of Alaska Press. Amy discovered our book, talked us into a fourth printing of the first edition, and pitched the second edition to University of Alaska Press. Her abiding enthusiasm is deeply appreciated.

Lastly, we thank Lynn Orbison of OK Publishing, our first publisher, for her unshakable faith in the book, for making the commitment to get it into print, and for proving it filled an important niche in the market.

Acknowledgments for the First Edition

If there was ever any doubt in our minds that a book doesn't happen by itself, this experience has more than proved it. This project was truly a joint effort. Numerous people helped throughout the process, from inception to completion. To all who gave us their time, knowledge, technical assistance, or moral support, we sincerely appreciate your contributions.

Our thanks go to John Ballard, Virginia Bedford, Philip Granberry, Cal Mercer, and Debra Van Stone for equipment and/or technical assistance; Larry Gilson, Lisa B. Fallgren Stevens, and Cal White for technical and photographic support; Will, Lori, and Dan Howard for participating in a photographic session for the book; and Polly Walter for designing, producing, and taking most of the photographs for *Skijoring: An Introduction to the Sport*, the booklet that started it all.

Kathy Frost, Cal Mercer, and Leslie Barber Noyes reviewed the initial book outline and made suggestions for improvement. The manuscript was reviewed and critiqued, in whole or in part and in various stages, by Richard Burrows DVM, Susan Butcher, Rich Fox, Kathy Frost, Kent Karns, Karl Kassel, Linda Leonard, and Chris McCaleb. Jim Arthurs and Chris McCaleb assisted with the section on first aid. Our sincere thanks to Susan Butcher and David Monson for fitting the Foreword into their hectic schedules.

Ken Ulz at Kobuk Feed Company allowed Carol to work on the book during company time (although this book was also completed in spite of him!).

George Rae enthusiastically supported the writing of this edition from the very beginning. Bob Levorsen provided much-appreciated information on international dog-driving events. Jim Welch's interest in the project came at an opportune time and rejuvenated the authors' efforts to find a publisher. A special thanks to Sally Atwater for asking the right questions.

Unflagging personal encouragement, moral support, and occasionally life support were provided by a host of people, among them Steve Carwile, Kay Fox, Rich Fox, Prescott Hazeltine, Allen and Louise Kaynor, Cal Mercer, Ruth Morgan, Leslie Barber Noyes, and Dale Raitto.

Portions of the book are based on articles written for *Mushing* magazine. The chapter on trail etiquette grew out of material provided by the Alaska Dog Mushers Association and the Alaska Skijoring and Pulk Association. The chapter on skijoring with children and people with disabilities was based in part on information provided in the Fjellpulken catalog put out by Rustadstuen Pulkfabrikk of Lillehammer, Norway. Much of the philosophical material was based on Carol's senior thesis at Vermont College for her undergraduate degree, for which she would like to thank her advisor, Dick Herrmann, and the entire staff of the Adult Degree Program.

Heidi Barker started out as an illustrator, became a friend and partner in the project, and turned out to be a perceptive editor as well. Thanks also go to Dick Kaynor, who edited the book in his almost-nonexistent spare time.

We would like to thank Lynn Orbison, our publisher, for taking a chance on us and for demonstrating her commitment to this project in a manner that defies description.

Foreword

Skijoring is a great sport. You don't need a kennel, a husky, or even a sled to be able to enjoy the pleasure of working with your dog in the winter. All sizes, shapes, and breeds of dogs can be used to pull you on skis. Skijoring will keep your dog fit, happy, and healthy.

Skijor With Your Dog gives you all the information you need to get started in this exciting sport. Whether you throw yourself into competitive skijoring or take your family pet around the block for fun, it has a great deal to offer. I have always believed that respect, love, and understanding are the basis for a good philosophy of dog training and care. This book not only advocates that philosophy but provides easily understood information on the ins and outs of skijoring.

It takes a special kind of teamwork to win a race. Great teams don't just happen; they are built of distinctly different dogs working together with their musher. I have always treated each dog as an individual, able to communicate many things about its health and needs. I use this information to understand and work with dogs to help them become powerful members of the team. Mari Høe-Raitto and Carol Kaynor have emphasized dogs as teachers as well as students. This is an invaluable basis for learning to enjoy your dog and skijoring.

Even now, with 130 dogs in my kennel, I still go out and hook up a couple of dogs to skijor with for the pure enjoyment of the sport. I hope you find your experience with it as gratifying.

Susan Butcher
Eureka, Alaska
1991

Preface

In the mid-1980s, when most of us skijorers were backyard types who held leashes or tow bars in our hands, Mari Høe-Raitto appeared in Fairbanks with classy Norwegian skijoring equipment and a way of skiing so effortlessly that her skis seemed extensions of her feet. She proved to be a formidable competitor. When Mari entered a skijoring race, she usually won it. She was also a generous and patient teacher, always willing to answer questions and give helpful suggestions.

In 1985, Mari and I organized a skijoring race, the first of many joint efforts to promote the sport we both loved. Every time we worked together on a project—a skijoring clinic, a race, a television commercial, a talk show—I learned something more about skijoring and about dogs. My desire for knowledge was shared by numerous other skijorers who clamored for more information. I turned to Mari one day and said, "You know, we should write a book."

The chapters that follow are the result of our collaborative efforts as a professional dog driver and a professional writer, both of whom share an addiction to dogs. We owe a great deal to the teachers that have come before us. This book represents a compilation of not just our own knowledge, opinions, and philosophies but also a wealth of information shared by other dog owners and dog drivers.

Skijoring has come a long way since we wrote the first edition of this book in 1991. Its popularity has grown exponentially over the past twenty years, and it is becoming a familiar sport on both sides of the Atlantic. Other forms of dog driving also have grown in popularity all over the world. Along with the traditional form of dog mushing on snowy trails outside of cities, we've seen a rise in dog-powered sports in densely populated areas, sometimes called "urban mushing," and on surfaces other than snow, often called "dryland mushing." From canicross (being pulled on foot by a dog in harness) to bikejoring to being pulled on a scooter or other wheeled rig, people are finding many creative ways to harness the power of a hard-pulling dog.

With this rise in popularity, pretty much every aspect of dog-powered sports has seen advances—new equipment, more effective training techniques, better nutrition, and improved dog breeding programs. We've tried to pick and choose what might be most pertinent to the beginning skijorer. We've added a chapter that touches on a few different forms of dryland skijoring, but we agree with Miki and Julie Collins, authors of *Dog Driver: A Guide for the Serious Musher*: someone needs to write an entire book on dryland mushing.

Notes and Disclaimers

- We alternate the pronouns "he" and "she" in this book when referring to both dogs and people. It seems the simplest way to avoid neglecting one or the other half of the population.
- We have occasionally used name brands in this book to describe certain products. In no case should this be taken as an endorsement. We neither endorse nor recommend any product named in the following chapters.
- Skijoring is fun and exciting, but like many such sports, it carries the potential for injury. We have tried to emphasize safety and control throughout this book, but we cannot

guarantee you'll never be injured while skijoring. Skijoring also carries the potential for driver miscalculations that result in less-than-optimal outcomes. Common sense is the responsibility of the reader.

- Consult your veterinarian before implementing any recommendations for dog care made in this book. We are not qualified to offer clinical medical advice, and our suggestions are not meant to take the place of professional veterinary care. We have tried to emphasize and promote the welfare of the dog throughout these chapters because we believe that health and well-being should be paramount in any human-canine interaction, whether the dog is your family pet or a full working partner.

- This book is meant to be as comprehensive as possible, but it can't possibly cover every possible angle of skijoring. To do so, we would have had to write a twelve-pound book—and you would have had to buy one of those book pedestals that encyclopedic dictionaries sit on. We tried to cover as many important points as possible without overly duplicating what's been said elsewhere.

- You may notice references to competition throughout the book. A little bias in this direction was inevitable, since both of us have been involved in competitive dog driving for many years.

We hope this new edition will continue to provide beginning skijorers with a good base of information from which to launch into the dog-driving world, as well as give experienced skijorers new tips and tricks. Whether novice or expert, we wish you exceptional dogs, unbreakable skis, and challenging trails.

Carol Kaynor
Fairbanks, Alaska
1991 and 2011

1

Dog Driving With Skis

Skiing behind your dog in harness is the perfect winter activity if you like to ski and your dog loves to run. With a pair of skis, a little bit of extra equipment, and a dog that likes to pull, you have everything you need to enjoy a snowy winter trail. Skijoring allows you to experience the speed and pleasure of dog mushing on a smaller, more economical scale. Almost anyone—of nearly any age—can learn how to skijor.

The sport of skijoring (a Norwegian word that translates literally as "ski driving") is elegantly simple: A dog in harness tows a skier by a line that is either handheld or attached to a special extra-wide belt worn by the skier. Most skijorers limit their dog power to one or two dogs, with three dogs customarily the maximum. With more than three dogs, any gain in power or speed is usually counteracted by the possibility of tangles or lack of adequate control. Either cross-country or downhill skis can be worn, but cross-country skis are more commonly used so that the skier can help the dog by striding or skating.

All sorts of breeds—from Labrador retrievers to poodles to Irish wolfhounds—have pulled skiers. Skijoring dogs can weigh anywhere from thirty pounds to more than one hundred pounds. Most dogs have a natural instinct to pull, so the family pet is almost as likely to take to the sport as is a racing sled dog. A skijoring team can travel surprisingly long distances, depending on the type of dog and the skier's ability. A single dog can pull a competent skier up to thirty miles a day, but many skijorers are just as happy to take their house pet on a one-mile jaunt. The primary requirement for successful skijoring, just as it is for obedience and fieldwork, is a close relationship between dog and owner.

Skijoring is easy to learn. Some cross-country skiing ability is necessary, but you needn't be an expert skier to enjoy the sport. Nor does your dog have to be in top condition, as long as you operate within the dog's limits and abilities. Skijoring helps skiers to develop balance and is wonderful, fun exercise for the dog.

Where Did Skijoring Come From?

The domesticated dog traveled beside us long before the earliest recorded history of humans. Beginning with the first friendships between people and dogs, which may have developed more than thirty thousand years ago, the dog's purpose has varied with time and place. Dogs have been our hunters, companions, guardians, workers, guides, and more. We've asked them to perform an incredible variety of tasks, and they have proven adaptable enough to mold themselves into almost anything we wish them to be. One task for which they have proven admirably suited has been to pull people and gear across the frozen regions of the Far North. The domestic dog's role in arctic transportation reaches back at least twelve thousand years.

Dog mushing originated with the people who lived along the coasts of Siberia, Alaska, Canada, and Greenland. Dog teams were a necessary means of survival for hunters and trappers and later played an essential role in arctic exploration. Dog mushing in these areas has evolved into the style most Americans are familiar with today: three to twenty dogs pull a sled ridden by the driver.

Skijoring is a hybrid sport, combining the principles of skiing and dog mushing. Its history ranges across the arctic coasts, where dog mushing evolved, and Scandinavia, the birthplace of skiing. The practice may stretch all the way back to the Yuan and Ming dynasties in China, 1271–1644. In *The Culture and Sport of Skiing: From Antiquity to World War II*, E. John B. Allen quotes from a history of Chinese skiing: "tens of dogs pull a person on a pair of wooden boards…galloping on the snow and ice faster than a horse." The Sámi of Scandinavia may have skijored behind reindeer centuries ago, and even today, skijoring races with reindeer are held in Tromsø, Norway, as part of the Sámi Days festival. But

Skijoring has been practiced in Alaska for a hundred years or more. This photo, titled "Dog teaming on skis, great sport in Alaska," was taken around 1912.

it is likely that the modern, popular form of skijoring behind dogs has its roots in the gold rush.

Scandinavian Ski Driving

The Scandinavian gold miners, trappers, and polar explorers who returned from the gold fields of North America took the idea of dog mushing back home with them. Large teams of dogs were impractical in their more highly populated countries, so they took their great love of skiing and teamed it up with a more modest version of Alaska-style (also known as Nome-style) mushing. The result was Nordic-style mushing, in which a team of one to four dogs pulls a small sled called a *pulk* (or *pulka*), with the driver skiing behind the sled.

In Scandinavia and the rest of Western Europe, skijoring developed as a training technique for Nordic-style mushing, rather than as a separate sport. Until very recently, skijoring competitions were rare in most European countries, and Nordic-style races for years outnumbered Alaska-style events. Yet in North America, Nordic-style mushing was virtually unknown until the mid-1980s.

Today, four major types of Nordic-style mushing exist in Norway: competition, touring, rescue work, and transportation for people with disabilities. While races are immensely popular, they are only one reason for the sport's popularity. The addition of dogs greatly enhances ski touring. Because a dog usually can pull its own weight in gear, touring with dogs increases the comfort and safety of the traveler. And, of course, the dogs are good company.

Nordic-style dog mushing plays an important part in rescue work in Norway, even in this era of high technology. Snowmachines and helicopters can travel almost anywhere, yet places still exist where only a dog team can go in cases of emergency. Motorized vehicles are not allowed in many Norwegian parks, for instance, so Nordic-style rescue teams provide emergency response there.

Most dog-driving clubs in Norway have volunteers who take people with disabilities out into the wilderness. Special pulks with windshields and thick padding transport adults in comfort. The outings offer a break from the usual confinement of winter but without the noise and impersonal nature of a snowmachine. The passenger in the sled has a feeling of being part of a team, as well as a feeling of freedom.

Skijoring in North America

Early Alaskans also combined skiing with dog sledding. But instead of exchanging the dogsled for a pulk, they took away the sled altogether and simply skied behind a dog. Trappers checked some of their shorter traplines this way. Early freighters and mail carriers also skijored behind dog teams and even skied in front of their dogsleds, using a steering pole called a *gee pole* (soft *g*) to guide the sled.

Down in the Lower Forty-eight (as Alaska residents call the forty-eight contiguous states of the United States), Scandinavian

Two drivers on skis accompany a freight team leaving Allakaket, Alaska, on the Detroit Arctic Expedition, circa 1926. The skier in front is using a gee pole.

ALASKA STATE LIBRARY, ALEXANDER MALCOLM SMITH PHOTOGRAPH COLLECTION, ASL-P136-23

immigrants introduced the sport of skijoring more than a hundred years ago when they brought their love of skiing with them to North America. At that time, it was more common to go for a wild skijoring ride behind a horse, at least while horses were still the primary method of transportation. Allen's history mentions skijoring behind a horse as a popular winter activity for the wealthy in both Europe and North America in the 1920s. People also skijored behind snowmachines, cars, and even airplanes. Horse-skijoring competitions are still immensely popular in some areas today.

In the mid-1980s, skijoring with dogs began to catch people's attention all over North America. This is perhaps because of the rise in popularity of cross-country skiing, dog mushing, and pet ownership in general. As an ideal way for both pet and owner to get outdoor exercise, skijoring has become a popular pastime. More and more people—from Maine to Virginia, from Alaska to California, all across the northern states and Canada—are taking to the skijoring trail. In places with little or no snow, several different forms of "dryland skijoring" have become popular, such as canicross (running behind a dog in harness), bikejoring, and being pulled on a scooter, light cart, or three-wheeled rig.

So What's the Big Deal?

What is behind skijoring's popularity? Excitement and adventure are two good reasons. A fast skijoring team can easily top twenty miles per hour—that's a mile in just three minutes. Using a dog, a skier can travel greater distances with ease and can explore backcountry trails without lugging a heavy backpack. For those downhill skiers who think cross-country skiing is too much work for too little excitement, being pulled by a dog is like having your own personal rope tow, but better. You can't train a rope tow to wait for you if you fall.

Dog owners receive a great deal of satisfaction and pleasure from working closely with their dogs. Skijoring offers terrific opportunities to nurture this relationship. It's hard to describe the pleasure of seeing your canine friend dance in excitement whenever he sees his harness, or the thrill of four-legged power when your dog charges off the starting line in a race.

Mushing is the ultimate indulgence for some dog lovers, but it can be expensive when you add up dog food, sledding equipment, and veterinary bills for a dog team. Skijoring requires as little as a single dog, a pair of skis, a harness, a belt, and a line. This makes it a great introduction to the joys of running dogs.

belt (with quick-release snap or open hook)

line

harness

Skijoring and Dog Mushing: What's the Difference?

Skijoring and Alaska-style dog mushing share many similarities. The same or a similar type of harness for the dog and some of the same equipment is used; the most significant difference is the skijorer's belt. The commands are virtually the same, as are the training techniques. Perhaps the single most important difference between skijoring and dog mushing is the role of the driver.

In dog mushing, the driver stands on the runners of a dogsled, steers the sled by weight and the handlebar, and uses a brake and snow hook to stop the dog team. The driver can help the team somewhat by running behind the sled or by pedaling (pushing with one foot), but the dogs do the bulk of the work.

Skijorers can help the dogs to a greater degree than a musher can. By striding, double poling, or skating, the skijorer becomes a true working member of the team and, if ambitious and strong enough, can work just about as hard as the dogs.

Whether going on a Sunday outing or engaging in serious competition, some basic skiing ability is essential for skijoring. Maintaining one's balance on skis takes more effort and attention than that needed to stay on sled runners. The skijorer constantly compensates for every turn, bump, and irregularity on the trail. Lacking a brake, the skijorer can stop in one of three ways: snowplow to a halt, stop the team by voice command alone, or sit down.

This illustrates the importance of voice commands in skijoring. Mushers often place little or no emphasis on teaching their dogs to "whoa," but most skijorers, lacking a brake, teach their dogs to stop and stand on command. Their only other choice is to learn to get back on their feet on the fly, because even the best of skiers will fall while skijoring.

Skijoring has many advantages over Alaska-style dog mushing. A large kennel is not required; even just one well-conditioned dog can pull a skier for many miles or race down a four-mile sprint track in less than twenty minutes. Skis are more portable than a dogsled, and a one-dog or two-dog team can fit in a car. And, as we've mentioned before, skijoring is relatively inexpensive.

Of course, dog mushing has advantages, too. The shortcomings of an individual dog are much less noticeable in a bigger team. Alaska-style mushing is physically less demanding and more forgiving for

DAVE PARTEE

those of us who weren't born on skis. You can travel farther and carry more gear with a dogsled. Dog mushers can go camping with almost anything they feel like taking, including a heavy canvas tent, a wood-burning stove, and several weeks' worth of food.

Despite some of the differences, the two sports are wonderfully compatible. A musher who also skis can use skijoring as an invaluable training tool. Because the relationship between skijorer and dog is so intimate, it can be an excellent way to work with problem dogs or to train leaders. For the novice dog driver, skiing behind one or two dogs can serve as an excellent introduction to dog mushing. Or skijoring can stand on its own as one more way to get the very most out of winter.

2

Teaching Yourself to Skijor

Obviously, you should know how to ski before you begin skijoring. But how much skiing skill do you need? Do you have to be an expert skier? It depends. If you plan to race competitively, or if you intend to use fast, powerful sled dogs that don't have the foggiest idea what *easy* or *whoa* means, then you'd better be a very good skier indeed. If you plan to skijor with a family pet that pulls at a slow trot, you won't need nearly the same skill level.

Regardless of your plans, rudimentary skiing skills are a necessity for skijoring. If you don't know how to ski, you can quickly burn out your dog with frequent stops, jerks, and falls. And if in your learning stages you fall on your dog or frighten him, he may not want to skijor again.

Norwegians are said to be "born on skis" because they are steeped from birth in an environment of skiing. If you grow up watching people ski all the time, you will learn without formal instruction. But if you are an adult and have never skied before, we recommend you take a class, read books on cross-country skiing, or find someone to teach you the basics. As in learning anything, skiing is a lot easier if someone can show you what you are doing wrong or right. A few structured lessons can advance you further than if you try to teach yourself, and they can save both you and your dog a lot of frustration. Check with ski shops for names and addresses of ski clubs or instructors in your area. Ski-shop personnel may also be able to recommend helpful instructional books.

Skiing takes a bit of motivation to learn. It will help immensely if you enjoy being out in the snow, can tolerate getting a little cold at times, and have the gumption to keep at it. Just about anybody can learn to ski with a little time, patience, and good instruction. We will give you a few pointers here to get you started, but they aren't meant to take the place of formal instruction. Please keep in mind that we can't teach you to ski in this one short chapter.

Basic Skills

Balance

For both skiing and skijoring, balance is the first and most important skill to develop. Balance is the ability to feel at ease on your skis and is essential to handling bumps, turns, and slopes comfortably. With good balance, you can confidently meet changes in terrain.

If you've been dancing, biking, kayaking, or doing any other activities that require good balance, you'll be starting out ahead when you learn to ski. The most important point for maintaining balance is to stay relaxed. You also need to learn where your center of gravity should be.

To develop balance skills, it's better to start out without poles. When children begin skiing lessons, the instructor or parent usually has them ski without poles for the first two or three years. This helps them to develop a feel for where their center of gravity lies in various situations. They learn to rely on their body—instead of the poles—for balance.

To practice balance, choose a flat trail and glide as far you can on each ski (without poles), trying to keep your balance as you keep your weight on the gliding ski. Once you feel comfortable on flat trails, begin to broaden your skills by skiing on all types of terrain—downhill, uphill, sidehill, bumpy, soft snow, ice—so that when you start skijoring, you'll be prepared for the occasional surprises that are sure to crop up.

Falling

Part of developing balance includes learning how to fall. Falling correctly is an essential skill. Even the best skiers take a spill now and then, and skijoring is especially conducive to falling. For kids, falling usually is no problem. Children automatically relax when they fall, and a relaxed fall is less likely to hurt. But adults often tighten up when they fall and can end up with sore muscles and bruises or even a broken limb.

SIBERPOP PHOTOGRAPHY

This racing skijorer was just short of the finish line when she fell, but she recovered nicely and went on to finish well.

Falling is what the ski schools teach you first. There's no substitute for actual experience, so they start by having you stand up and then fall down. (Really!) Try it. Once again, the main point is to relax. Practice falling easily, without tensing up. Be careful not to put your arms out rigidly to break your fall. Your outstretched arm can twist or even break from the impact unless you allow it to give way gently with the force. It goes against instinct, but it is much safer to take a fall in a tuck position, with your shoulder or side bearing the brunt of the impact.

Avoid falling directly forward or backward. If you fall forward, you may bruise yourself on the tips of your skis, and if you are skijoring, you may get dragged forward on your face. (This is called a "face-plant.") If you fall straight back, you may injure your tailbone or jar your back. It's best to fall sideways if possible.

If a fall is inevitable, don't fight it. If you realize that you're about to take an unavoidable spill, direct your weight sideways and control the fall as much as possible. But once you've begun to master the technique of falling, it's best to avoid doing so when you can. Anticipating a spill can make you fall needlessly.

Beginning skiers sometimes use falling as a way of stopping. It may be a quick and easy way to halt forward motion, but it is an extremely bad habit for aspiring skijorers to develop. It's easy to burn out a skijoring dog by falling; both Carol and Mari have done so. The fall jerks on the dog's back and can be an unpleasant, even frightening, experience for her, especially if you end up falling on top of her. The dog will also get just plain tired of your falling.

As you learn how to fall down, you'll also need to learn how to get back up. This is not always as easy as it might seem, particularly if you fall on a slope with your skis pointing uphill. Before you try to get up, lie on your back and swing your skis up in the air, then pivot your body around until your skis are pointing sideways along the slope. If you point your skis straight uphill or downhill, they will slip right out from under you as soon as you put your weight on them.

Don't forget that your ultimate goal is to have a dog pulling you, and that dog may not stay still while you struggle back to your feet. It's a good idea to become accomplished at both falling and getting up before you add a dog to the equation.

Stopping and Slowing Down

The snowplow is the most basic method of decreasing your speed or coming to a halt. To snowplow, bend your legs and slide the backs of your skis outward, with your ski tips almost together but not crossing. The wider the angle of your skis, the slower you will go. Bending your knees more deeply will increase the edge on your skis, which also will help you to go slower.

As with learning balance, it is best to start without poles when you learn to slow and stop. Your body weight should be back on your heels, not on your toes. Don't lean forward. Your arms

DAVE PARTEE

should be relaxed and hanging by your side, your back straight and your body relaxed.

Turning

The snowplow also can be used to make turns. When you come into a turn, put your weight on the inside edge of the outer ski (usually the ski that is downhill). Bend your knees, keep your body upright, and avoid leaning forward. The outer knee actually moves inward to dig the inside edge of the ski into the snow. Even when you take a turn with your skis parallel, your knees will point in toward the turn.

Reversing Direction

What if you want to stop and reverse direction? The simplest way to do so is called the "star turn." To execute a star turn, gradually step your skis around in a circle until you're facing in the opposite direction. In another popular method called a "Lapp turn," lift one ski up and turn it in the opposite direction, using your poles

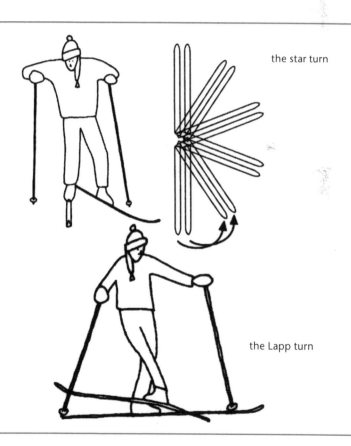

the star turn

the Lapp turn

for stability. After you put that ski down and firmly place your weight on it, move the other ski around. The Lapp turn is faster than the star turn, but if you are not an experienced skier, the star turn is easier.

Skiing Techniques

In cross-country skiing, there are essentially three techniques for creating forward motion: diagonal striding, skating, and double poling. Beginning skiers and skijorers usually learn the more traditional diagonal stride; racers tend to focus on skating. Competitive skijorers need to learn both techniques, as well as double poling. The pointers that follow are meant to supplement other instruction; if you don't know how to diagonal ski or to skate, please don't try to learn simply by reading these paragraphs.

Diagonal Striding

Diagonal skiing or striding is so called because your arms and legs move diagonally to each other. Glide on your left ski while reaching out with your right arm and pole, then glide on your right ski and reach out with your left arm and pole. While you eventually will want the added power of the pole thrusts, it is actually best to start out without poles. It can also be helpful to have someone critique your style. Having someone videotape you can help you master the skill. If you have never skied before, it can be difficult to tell whether you are skiing correctly until you actually experience the effortlessness of a well-executed diagonal stride.

Skating

To skate, put your weight on your right ski and glide diagonally forward on your left ski, transferring your weight to that left ski as you push off with the right ski. Then shift your weight to glide outward on the right ski, pushing off with the left. Skating on skis is similar to ice skating, but as Carol found out, ice-skating skills

may not translate directly into skate skiing. Try skating without poles at first so you don't become dependent on them. To practice your balance, skate long strokes on each ski (also without poles), keeping your weight on the ski you are gliding on.

Don't worry if skating initially seems difficult. Carol had learned to skate on ice when she was very young, but she didn't begin skiing until she was in her twenties. She learned the diagonal stride easily but had a lot of trouble learning to skate. She had two problems: she depended too much on her poles and thus didn't learn where her weight should go; and whenever she got tired, she automatically slipped into diagonal mode in the middle of a skating stride—a guaranteed way to lose one's balance.

After becoming so discouraged that she considered giving up, Carol happened to go skijoring one day without poles. (She was training a new dog and didn't want the poles to distract him.) On a whim, she casually tried a few skating strokes. Minus both the poles and the pressure, the skating stride finally made sense to her, and she learned a rudimentary skating technique that worked well behind a steadily pulling dog. She was still not very good at skating without a dog, however. An excellent ski instructor evaluated her technique and pinpointed what she needed to work on.

Double Poling

Whether you compete or skijor just for fun, double poling is an excellent way to assist your dog. To double pole, reach out with both poles at the same time, keeping your skis parallel. Stretch your arms out in front of you, plant your poles, and in a smooth movement, pull yourself forward. As you pull, let your upper body bend almost in half and use your body weight to give the stroke more power. Be sure to follow through with a strong push. Bend your knees a little as you bring your arms back in front of you, and then straighten up in preparation for the next double-pole stroke.

Comparing these three techniques, skating is unquestionably the best for sustained speed. Diagonal skiing may seem archaic for competition, but if you find yourself on a narrow trail where skating is impossible, diagonal skiing and double poling may be the only way you can help your dog. If you race with fast dogs, you can sometimes benefit more from a strong double-poling technique than from skating behind the dog. Whether skating helps or slows down a fast dog depends a great deal on your dog's ability and on your technique.

Skiing on Uneven Terrain

Uneven terrain can be a real challenge for a beginner. On bumpy trails, your legs should be slightly bent in the low spots and much more bent in the high spots, so that your center of gravity stays almost level. Let your knees act as shock absorbers. On sidehill runs (when you are moving across a slope, rather than down it),

keep your weight on the downhill ski. The tip of the upper ski should be half a foot ahead of the tip of the downhill ski. Your knees should be bent slightly in toward the hill. To practice, lift your upper ski and just ski on the downhill ski. This will also help your balance.

Skijoring Goals

Keep these points in mind when you learn to ski:

- Don't use poles at first.
- Try to develop a feel for the placement of your weight, your center of gravity, and your balance.
- Aim to ski smoothly, without apparent effort.

With a little practice, you'll be able to skijor comfortably behind your dog without injuring yourself or terrorizing your dog. Whether you intend to poke around your backyard or travel into the backcountry, it's important that you feel relaxed and confident on skis. If you are nervous, your dog will pick up on your fear and may not perform well.

In this mass-start race, skijorers were required to forgo ski poles. Being able to skate well without them offered a distinct competitive edge.

If your objective in learning to skijor is to take your dog around the block twice a week, don't be intimidated by the image of competitive skijorers in sleek Lycra suits and on hot racing skis. You certainly don't need to purchase lots of fancy equipment. The skis in your closet probably will do just fine. Likewise, you won't need to learn all the subtle variations of the skating technique. Later on, if your goals and ambitions warrant it, you might want to invest in a different pair of skis and some advanced instruction for mountain touring or for competition.

If you do want to compete, start at the beginning by developing balance and work up gradually to competition-level skills. If you plan to go on tours, know how to ski on uneven terrain, on ice and overflow (water that seeps up over ice), on sidehills, and in any other types of conditions you may encounter. Choose trips commensurate with your skiing skills and your dog's ability, so that your experiences—and those of your dog—remain positive. Be sure you are physically in shape before you go on longer trips, and make sure your dog is well conditioned, too.

Our basic philosophy about learning to skijor is this: Don't try to do more than your physical abilities will allow, or aim so high that you guarantee failure. Remember not to ask more of your dog than he's ready to give. The most important thing is for both of you to enjoy what you're doing.

3

Equipment

One of the great beauties of skijoring is how inexpensive it is to get started. Assuming you already have skis, you can purchase a good-quality belt, skijoring line, and harness for the dog for less than $100. But there are some basic points to keep in mind when you decide to outfit yourself. Skijoring can be made significantly easier or harder by the type of equipment you use. The wrong kind of equipment can be downright disastrous. More expensive does not always mean well suited, but quality is important.

Outfitting the Skier

Skis

One of the most common questions asked by beginning skijorers is, "What kind of skis should I use?" The simple answer is any kind of skis you feel comfortable with. A few people have even used downhill skis, particularly if they are running multidog teams. But most skijorers use cross-country skis because they offer both flexibility and control, and they allow the skier to work behind the dog.

If you are just starting out, the skis in your closet will probably do just fine. If you're in the market for new skis, talk to the folks at your local sporting goods store, flip through some ski magazines, and, if possible, talk to other skijorers before you buy. If you want to buy skis specifically for skijoring, there are several considerations to keep in mind. The kind of skijoring you will do most often (which might be racing, backcountry touring, or short jaunts for fun) and the trails you will do it on (which might be groomed, ungroomed, narrow, wide, hilly, flat, icy, or snowy) will affect the kind of ski that works best for you.

Skating skis are usually shorter and a little narrower than touring skis. Skating skis are great on groomed trails, especially those that are wide and flat. Shorter skis increase your control and maneuverability. If you use ungroomed trails, a pair of longer touring skis might be the best bet. You might consider a binding system that locks down at the heel when traveling in steep terrain. Backcountry trails or steep terrain might seem to call for metal-edged skis, but this type carries the risk of injury if you strike your dog with the skis. If you feel you absolutely must have the added control of metal edges, look for skis that have metal on the sides but not the tips or the tails. Never use metal-edged skis on any outing or in any race in which you have any chance of contacting or passing someone else's dog.

There are more opinions about the best type of ski than there are types of skis, as you'll find out if you talk to other skijorers, join a skijoring e-mail list, or talk to skijoring outfitters. Please keep the safety of the dog uppermost in your mind, especially when listening to discussions about metal-edged skis. Remember that no matter how good a skier you might be, you can't control the actions of other skijorers and their dogs.

Poles

Not all types of ski poles work well for skijoring. Bamboo ski poles in particular break too easily for the kind of abuse skijoring is sure to give them. Aluminum poles are good because they are durable and inexpensive. Lightweight carbon-fiber poles are popular with some competitive skijorers, but they are more expensive.

Your skiing style and your preferences dictate what length of ski pole to buy. If you skate, you'll probably want longer poles; if you use the diagonal stride, you'll need shorter ones. Some skijorers

DAVE PARTEE

develop a distinct preference for a particular length, regardless of their chosen ski technique. Unless you are competitive and wish to have the optimum length for speed and power, the bottom line is to go with the length that feels most comfortable to you.

Boots

Because of the decreased activity and added wind chill of skijoring, you will probably need warmer footgear than the average cross-country skier. Consider investing in well-insulated boots or a pair of ski-boot covers. The boots you purchase must be compatible with your binding system. If you are buying a ski package (skis, boots, and poles) and don't know which bindings to choose, the best advice we can pass on is to focus on the boots. Your feet do the most work and carry your weight besides, so a well-fitting, comfortable boot is absolutely essential. Skate and classic boots are seldom warm, so boot size should accommodate thick socks without squeezing or binding up. One of Murphy's laws says that

DAVE PARTEE

the most comfortable boot for you will also be the most expensive. If at all possible, grit your teeth and ignore the price. On the other hand, less expensive models in a line often are warmer than top-of-the-line race boots.

As with skis, the type of boot you need will be impacted by the kind of skijoring you plan to do. If you plan to skate on groomed trails, you'll need a skating boot. If you'll be going on long tours or traveling the backcountry, you might be most comfortable in a well-insulated high-top boot.

Boot Covers

If your feet get cold easily, ski-boot covers may make the difference between comfort and misery or even frostbite. Depending on the type of ski bindings used, boot covers either slip over the boot like an oversock or wrap around it with Velcro fasteners. Boot covers cut the wind and keep out the snow, and a good pair can extend your foot's comfort range by fifteen degrees or more. Ultra-thin insulating material, such as Thinsulate or Thermolite, boosts the effectiveness of boot covers even more. If you don't want to spend the money but suffer from cold toes, try using a pair of old wool socks cut to fit around your bindings.

DAVE PARTEE

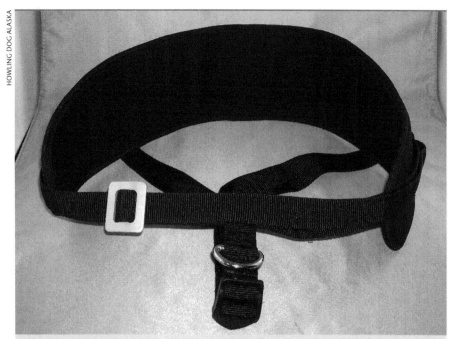

This skijoring belt fastens around the hips to eliminate pressure on the spine. Careful adjustment of the leg straps keep the pulling force low. A belt with a wide back and lower pulling force is much more comfortable than one that rides up around the waist.

Belts

There's absolutely no substitute for a decent skijoring belt. You may prefer to hold the skijoring line in your hand, but sooner or later you'll find yourself on a flat or slightly uphill trail with a tired dog, and you'll discover why most of us use a belt. Can you imagine double poling with a skijoring line in your hand? For that matter, imagine putting your foot back into a ski binding while your dog keeps pulling on the hand that holds the line. (This is one of many reasons why skijorers should consider obedience classes for their dogs, or at least should teach their dogs to stand still.)

Use a proper belt for skijoring. The belt must be *at least three inches wide* (about seven and a half centimeters) across your back, so that it covers at least two vertebrae. This is extremely important.

This minimum width decreases the possibility of injuries. With a narrower belt, you may hurt your back if you fall, come to a sudden stop, or are jerked forward unexpectedly by your dogs. The belt can be narrower in front. In fact, the older style of Norwegian leather belts used for skijoring and Nordic-style mushing are just that: wide in back, narrow in front, with a dual set of buckles (one on each side) for the best fit.

Several different styles of skijoring belt are available through mail order, and occasionally through local feed or sporting goods stores. Many belts are made of padded nylon or Cordura with or without leg straps. A belt without leg straps is simpler to put on, but it may slip up your back when worn against a nylon parka. Leg loops will anchor the belt down around the hips. A climbing harness can work as well as a skijoring belt, and those who use them

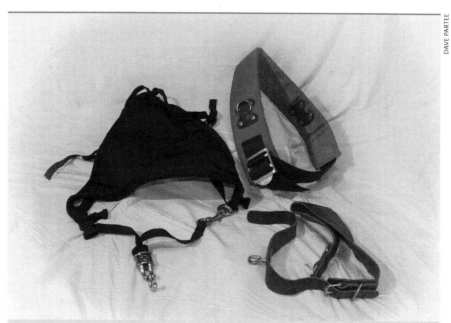

Clockwise from left: A soft cloth belt with leg straps; a belt with dual rings designed to be used by a person pulling a pulk; and a Norwegian leather belt with open hook.

claim that climbing harnesses are both comfortable and effective. One outfitter we know of has designed a Cordura skijoring belt that includes a waist pack, a useful addition.

To some extent, the type of belt you use will be a matter of personal preference. Carol's favorite belt has a triangular shape in back that ends in adjustable waist and leg straps and has been fondly referred to as the "diaper" style. Mari's favorite is a leather belt she wears tightly around her waist, with a good quick-release clip.

We'd like to expand here on a point concerning belts versus handheld lines (such as leashes or tow bars). When Carol learned to skijor back in 1977, she held onto a leash attached to the dog's harness. Using a belt for the first time made her nervous. Wouldn't it throw her off balance? Wouldn't it be uncomfortable? Wouldn't she lose some control? She discovered that the answer to all three questions is *no*.

A side view of a triangular, soft cloth belt with leg straps.

A belt worn low around your waist (just above your hips) improves your balance because it transfers the pulling force to a point closer to your center of gravity. With a belt, you can ski comfortably from virtually any position—upright and relaxed, crouched low in a tuck, or bent forward at the waist while double poling. As long as the belt is wide enough and is worn low enough around your waist, it should not cause you any discomfort.

As for control, a belt expands your options rather than limiting them. Any time you feel the need to hold the line in your hand, it's right there for you to grab. Carol often holds the skijoring line when she's just starting out, to absorb the jolt of overeager dogs. When she has her skiing legs under her, she lets go again. It can also help to hold the line when going around sharp corners and over rough terrain.

Attach your skijoring line to your belt with a releasable clip, making sure the clip will stay with the belt—not go with the dog and line—when the line is released. (A bouncing piece of hardware attached to a loose and possibly frightened dog is not a good idea.) Some skijorers use a quick-release snap, also known as a panic snap. Look for high-quality and reliable hardware; you don't want the quick-release clip to release your dog unexpectedly. In Norway, the rule for skijoring and Nordic-style mushing is still an

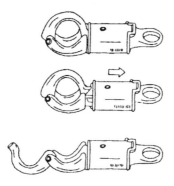

A quick-release snap in the shut and open positions. The snap is released by pulling back on the sleeve.

DAVE PARTEE

The leather belt with open hook is a style commonly used in Norway.

open hook, but skijorers in North America tend to prefer a closed releasable system.

There has been much debate over the years about quick releases and open hooks, and many skijorers disagree with their use. They argue that it's better not to risk losing your dog. We disagree. Our recommendation is still this: Whatever system you choose, don't permanently attach yourself to your dog. You will want the option of releasing your dog. For example, you (or your dog) may fall in a river, you may encounter a belligerent moose, or you may have a bad dogfight. You may get wrapped around a tree or another team in such a way that releasing the line is the only way to unwrap yourself. You may overtake your dog on a steep hill and end up shaped like a pretzel when he puts on the brakes.

A quick release also allows you to take the line off your belt and hold it in your hands when going down steep hills. If you fall at high speeds, you can avoid hurting both your dog and yourself by holding the line loose in your hands so you can let go of it quickly. If you have to let go of your dog, he should be trained to stop and stay on command.

One last caution: Some skijorers have been known to hold onto a snow hook attached to the dog's line so they can stop more easily. Please do not employ this method. Snow hooks are dangerous. If you are new to skiing and unable to snowplow to a stop, or your dogs are so unmanageable that you can't hold them without a brake, it's better to reduce the number of dogs you use than to depend on a potentially lethal piece of equipment such as a snow hook. Besides, using a snow hook to stop will jerk your dogs and could cause physical or emotional damage to them.

Clothing

Generally speaking, clothing suitable for cross-country skiing is also fine for skijoring. When you dress for skijoring, however, factor in the extra wind chill generated by the speed of your dog. Windproof clothing is recommended.

Outfitting the Dog

Harnesses

Skijorers nowadays have several choices besides the standard sled-dog racing harness. Don't buy a weight-pulling harness; it is not suitable for skijoring or mushing. Many skijorers use a regular X-back harness, which is the harness most commonly used by mushers. Some X-back harnesses have been modified specifically to fit the pointer and hound crossbreeds now common in the sled-dog world. The chest of a pointer crossbreed (also called a "cross") is often narrow and deep, and normal harnesses can slip to either side while the dog is running. Another choice is a short pulling harness, which looks like an X-back in the front but ends halfway down the dog's back. Short harnesses designed specifically for the sharper angle of a skijoring line work very well, and are especially good for tall skiers and/or short dogs. This kind of harness is called a "biking harness" in Norway, and was originally made of leather.

Finding a harness that fits properly can be the most difficult part of outfitting your dog. Many skijorers use their house pets for dog power, and these shepherds, Labs, goldens, Newfies, Aussies, Heinz 57s, or whatevers are often built quite differently from a standard-issue husky. That means a standard-issue sled-dog harness may not fit correctly, no matter how many different sizes you try. If you find your dog has too long or too short a back, too shallow or too deep a chest, a delicate coat that requires double-thick padding, or any other trait that sabotages a proper fit, try a different style of harness or go for a custom-made harness. Many outfitters will make a harness to individual specifications. It's worth it to ensure your dog's comfort and pulling efficiency.

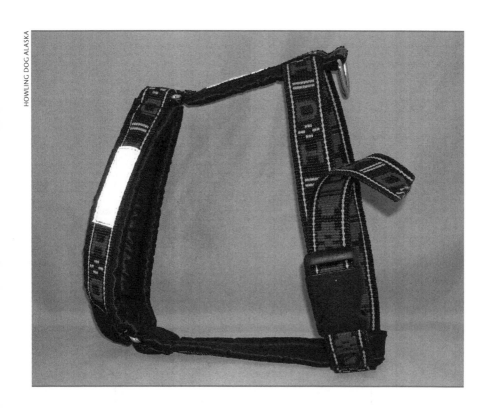

If you're brand-new to harnesses, you may be so daunted by the apparent complexity of the contraption that you can't even put it on the dog correctly, let alone determine a proper fit. It's easy to get the leg in the wrong hole, or put the head through the right place but miss the opening for the body. While figuring it all out, you may be trying to hold onto a squirming, wiggly canine who doesn't understand this silly mess of webbing any more than you do.

Take heart, and know that you're not alone. We all had to learn how to harness a dog, and rarely does anyone get it right on the very first try. You may find it helpful to study photos of dogs already harnessed. Look carefully at how the harness lies on the dog and which part goes where. If possible, persuade an experienced friend

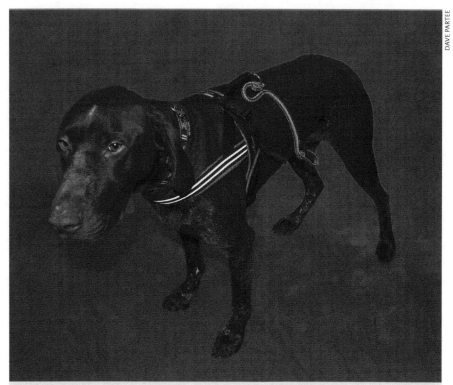

This harness, called a "buggy harness," works well for both skijoring and dog mushing.

to show you what to do. It's easier to watch someone else do it right and then have them coach you through your first attempt than to read and try to follow the instructions in this chapter. Also, remember that the process of being harnessed may intimidate the dog. Reassure the dog with your voice, take your time, and keep your temper at all costs.

Although most people instinctively try to put on a harness by stooping in front of the dog, it's actually easier to harness a dog by standing over his back, straddling his waist. From this position, you can anchor the dog with your legs to keep him from backing away from the harness. If the dog is on a chain, bring him to the end of the chain and face him inward, so that the chain becomes an opposing force should the dog try to back up.

The standard X-back harness is composed of a padded neck, a padded breastplate, underarm straps that go beneath the dog's forelegs, and crisscrossed straps that go over the dog's back. The first trick is to get the dog's head through two openings at once: the body opening and the neck opening. The easiest way to do this is to compress the harness so that the two openings become one. Fold the padded breastplate in half, so that you are holding each side of the neck opening together with each underarm strap. The V at the top of the breastplate (that is, the bottom of the neck opening) should be lined up with the V at the bottom of the breastplate (where the body opening starts).

Holding the harness thus compressed, and with the neck opening on top, slip it over the dog's head. If the dog is on a chain or leash, unclip the snap, pull the harness past the dog's collar, and reclip the snap. Pull the harness down the neck as far as it will go, pushing excess fur and skin up toward the dog's ears as you tug the harness lower. On a thickly furred dog, you'll have to snug down this part of the harness before you can get the legs through.

Now reach over, pick up one foreleg—bending the leg at the wrist so you don't strain it—and draw it through the underarm strap. Then do the same on the other side. Give the harness a firm tug from the back to set it on the dog's body.

Once you have the harness on and set, you can check for fit. Place your hand beneath the breastplate of the harness and feel for the dog's breastbone. The breastbone should meet the harness just beneath where the neck straps come together and make a V at the top of the breastplate. If the harness is too big, the breastbone will stick out the neck opening. If the harness is too small, the breastbone will fall below the joining of the neck straps. (Be sure that you've pulled the harness snugly down on the dog's neck before you check this part of the fit.)

If the chest fits, check the length. The end of the webbing should land right at the base of the dog's tail when the dog is pull-

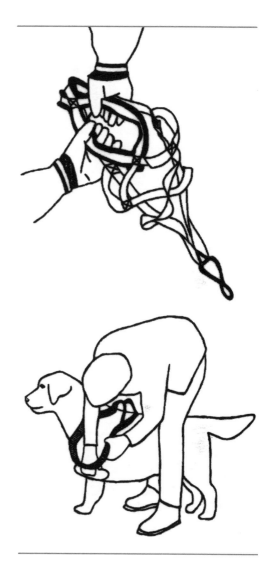

ing. Many harnesses naturally ride up on the dog's back until you apply backward pressure, so tug gently on the back of the harness when checking length. Make sure that the side straps don't fall over the dog's hindquarters, but run up from the belly just ahead of the hind legs. If the harness is too long and the side straps fall too far back, they can interfere with the motion of the hind legs. If the harness is too short or the straps run up too far forward, the straps may chafe the dog's sides or interfere with the running motion.

If your dog has an unusually short or long torso, you'll have a hard time finding a harness that fits both chest and length at once. If you are in a store that carries more than one make of harness, try a different brand. Harnesses are like clothes: sizing sometimes will vary enough between brands to accommodate a particular build. If that doesn't work, try a different style of harness. If you have no luck switching brands or styles, your best bet is to order a custom harness made to your dog's measurements but be sure to check the fit of the harness when it arrives. A poorly fitting harness can cause sores, ruin a dog's coat, or severely decrease the dog's comfort and pulling power. Don't settle for a marginal fit.

Skijoring Lines

Much more than just a leash or a dog-mushing tugline, a well-constructed skijoring line has a loop at one end that attaches to the belt's quick-release snap, a bungee section and a tugline section

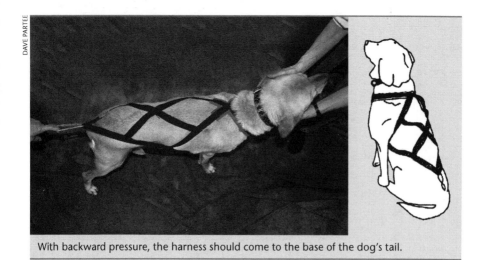

With backward pressure, the harness should come to the base of the dog's tail.

ending in a brass snap that attaches to the dog's harness. The entire line should be at least seven or eight feet long to prevent you from striking the dog with your skis, with fifteen or twenty feet being the maximum length.

Factors of terrain, power, and control determine the workable length for your skijoring line. If you skijor on hilly or uneven terrain, you may want to go with a longer length to give you a greater margin of error when your downhill speed threatens to overtake your dog. Also, the more power your dog has, the longer the bungee section can be. However, a longer line means less control for you. If you have a less well-behaved dog, you may need the extra control of a shorter line to cope with her antics.

Having a bungee cord (also known as a "shock cord") incorporated into the design is a requirement for skijoring. Once you have skijored with a bungee-cord line, we promise you won't want to go back. The bungee absorbs the shock of starting out with an excited dog. When you stride, skate, or double pole behind the dog, the bungee moderates the forward force and makes the

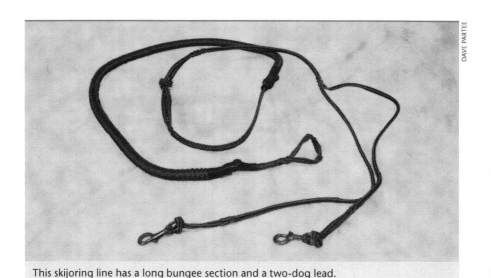

This skijoring line has a long bungee section and a two-dog lead.

process smoother for both you and the dog. If you fall, the bungee eases the stress of the abrupt halt—and if you fall at top speed, this is no small matter! Even while running smoothly, the bungee moderates the small jerks caused by the dog's natural gait, not only making your ride more comfortable but increasing the dog's comfort as well.

The bungee section of a skijoring line is usually made up of a length of poly rope about forty to sixty inches long, with bungee cord inserted into the core of the rope near one end. The bungee should be a stiff, winter-weight grade, one that has limited give and won't fall apart in extreme cold. The bungee cord should be between fifteen and twenty-five inches long (when not extended) and should be inserted into the portion of the line closest to your body, not closest to the dog.

Some skijoring lines are a one-piece affair, with a section of bungee followed by a basic tugline that clips into the dog's harness. We prefer lines constructed with a bungee section that ends in a loop or a sturdy metal O-ring, allowing separate tuglines to be attached to the bungee section. This type provides versatility. You can easily attach a one-, two-, or three-dog hitch to the loop or ring, ending up with three possible configurations off a single bungee section.

We recommend using an internal bungee cord (one that is woven into the core of the poly rope) rather than one that is attached to the outside of the rope. Speaking from personal experience, it's easy to catch a ski tip or a pole in the loops formed by an externally attached bungee. Also, avoid using cheap rubber bungees; they simply don't hold up under the stress and in cold temperatures. Be sure the bungee is securely anchored into the line and won't rip loose under stress. Later in this chapter, we describe how to make your own skijoring lines. Even if you decide to purchase a ready-made line, you might want to review that section so you'll know what design elements to look for.

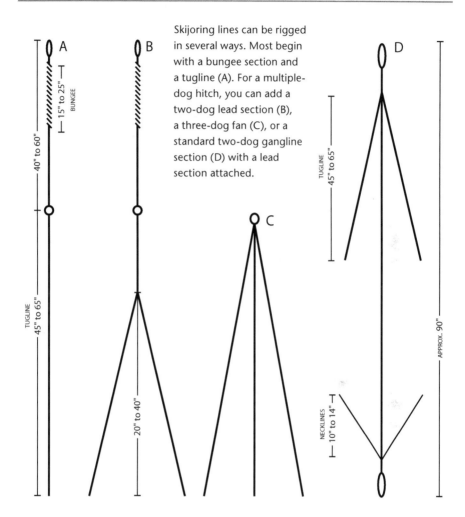

Skijoring lines can be rigged in several ways. Most begin with a bungee section and a tugline (A). For a multiple-dog hitch, you can add a two-dog lead section (B), a three-dog fan (C), or a standard two-dog gangline section (D) with a lead section attached.

The length of each component of your skijoring line is flexible, provided the line is long enough to keep your skis from interfering with the dog yet short enough to give you adequate control. We recommend a range of 7 to 15 feet.

Measurements here are roughly compatible with most dog-mushing equipment. To find skijoring lines, do a Web search or check the advertisements in mushing-related publications. Many skijoring outfitters sell lines in various configurations, and many mushing outfitters carry skijoring equipment as well.

DAVE PARTEE

Three dogs in a fan-style hitch without necklines.

How do you hitch two dogs to a skijoring line? As discussed earlier, this is easiest if the line is built in two sections. You can attach what's called a "two-dog lead," or you can run two single tuglines from the loop at the end of the bungee section. If you run three dogs in fan-style (three abreast), you simply add another tugline. If you want to run three dogs tandem-style, you can attach an Alaska-style gangline section to the bungee section and then run a one- or two-dog lead off the front of the gangline section. It's customary to run necklines from the gangline to the collars of the rear dogs, and some race rules require such necklines. Depending on how your dogs behave in a team, you may find that leaving off the necklines helps prevent tangles.

If you have a one-piece line, attaching more dogs becomes a greater challenge. Depending on how the line is constructed, you

This three-dog skijoring team is rigged with a two-dog lead section and a gangline section behind it for the third dog.

may be able to weave in or even tie in a second tugline. In the worst-case scenario, you'll have to purchase a second line.

Dog "Clothes"

A few extra items, such as booties, coats, crotch bands, or belly blankets, can increase the comfort of your dog if he has bad feet or a light coat. Dog booties slip over the dog's paws for protection against poor trail conditions or to prevent snowballs from forming between the dog's pads. A bootie also can be used to keep the dog from licking medication off an injured foot. Booties are made of several different materials; felt, Cordura, and polar fleece are three common types. The bootie attaches to the leg by means of a Velcro-fastened strip, which is sometimes elasticized. A bootie can save the dog's foot from injury, but it must be used with caution. If the fastener is pulled too tight, it can cut off circulation to the foot. The safest policy is to remove the bootie whenever you stop for

DAVE PARTEE

Dogs rarely enjoy wearing them at first, but booties can save a dog's feet from pain or injury under certain trail conditions.

more than a minute or two and to check the fit at regular intervals. It takes a little practice to find the balance between too tight and too loose.

Dog coats, crotch bands, and belly blankets protect a dog from harsh weather. A short-haired dog may need a full-coverage dog coat; a dog with a good coat on top but a sparsely coated belly may be able to get by with a belly blanket. Some dogs end up with frostbitten genitals and may require a crotch band. Short-haired dogs may also need a sleeping bag for overnight tours.

In the 1980s and 1990s, it was fairly unusual to see a skijorer's dog wearing a coat while working. But with the increased popularity of hound and pointer crossbreeds, running coats are becoming a common sight. If you have a hound- or pointer-cross sled dog, or a pet dog with a short coat, look for a coat specifically designed to be worn while pulling. Mari has found that dogs with shorter fur run a lot better with a windproof coat, starting at about ten degrees Fahrenheit above zero. They stretch out much better and she sees fewer muscle injuries.

Some coats go over the harness while others are put on underneath.

Finding Skijoring Equipment

If you're new to the world of dog driving, it may seem difficult at first to find sources for skijoring equipment. However, many retailers and outfitters across the United States carry dog-mushing and skijoring equipment. Ordering by mail is a little less desirable because you can't try on a harness or belt before you buy, but once you know what you want, you can choose between many reputable mail-order companies.

In Alaska, check feed and sporting goods stores; many carry dog-mushing supplies and skijoring equipment. Elsewhere, it's more common to order equipment through the mail. Equipment suppliers often advertise in *Mushing* magazine or at Sled Dog Central (http://sleddogcentral.com). A quick Web search on "skijor equipment" or "dog mushing supplies" also will give you many choices. Look for suppliers that specifically mention skijoring equipment. If you know a local dog musher or skijorer, pick that person's brains for equipment sources. Dog-mushing and skijoring clubs also may be able to suggest possible sources.

Making Your Own Equipment

Harnesses

Harnesses are relatively inexpensive and easy to find. Their designs are based on many years of research and experimentation. For these reasons, we don't recommend making your own harnesses. It likely will not be worth your time and effort, and it doesn't make sense to reinvent the wheel, especially when the issue is your dog's comfort and pulling efficiency.

Pulks

Commercially made pulks can be expensive. However, most commercial pulks will hold up far longer than the homemade variety, and since they are also used by skiers without dogs, they are available from many companies in both Europe and North America. If you don't plan to compete in Nordic-style races or do any serious touring, it's possible to fabricate a pulk out of an inexpensive plastic child's sled, although Mari does not recommend this. For more details on Nordic-style mushing and types of pulks, see chapter 9.

Skijoring Lines

Of the various accoutrements for skijoring, lines are the easiest to make yourself. In a pinch, even a simple leash will work. But a good skijoring line is much more than a leash.

A top-quality, functional skijoring line is not particularly difficult to put together. A few key techniques and measurements will ensure its effectiveness and endurance. Even if you decide to purchase a ready-made line, understanding how a well-constructed skijoring line is put together will give you a better idea of what to look for.

Recommended Materials

You need the following materials to make a one-dog skijoring line:

- Eighteen to twenty-four inches of ten-millimeter winter-weight bungee cord (or shock cord)
- Waxed heavy-duty thread and a large needle or sewing awl, or four number-three hog rings and hog ring pliers
- Two three-inch pieces of shrink wrap (usually found in the electrical section of hardware or department stores)
- Eight feet of three-eighths-inch braided polypropylene (poly) rope for main bungee section
- Four and a half feet of quarter-inch or three-eighths-inch braided poly rope for tugline section
- Three-eighths-inch fid (a hollow, pointed tool used to weave poly rope)
- Quarter-inch fid
- Half-inch fid
- Five-eighths-inch brass snap

Most of these materials can be found in feed, hardware, or lumber stores, or can be ordered through mushing equipment retailers and outfitters. The range of measurements given will allow you to customize your line. Some people like more spring in the line and therefore use a longer piece of bungee cord. You can also lengthen or shorten individual components (such as a shorter bungee section or a longer tugline) based on your individual preferences.

The Loop

Making a self-locking, nonslip loop in the poly rope probably is the most complicated part of the whole procedure. (If you think making the loop is tough, try *explaining* it!) The following instruction is for

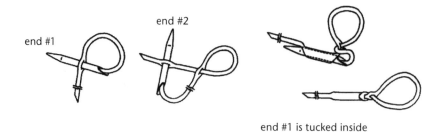

end #1   end #2

end #1 is tucked inside

one of the simplest methods; several other variations also will work. You may find that taking apart an already-constructed loop will help you learn how to make one.

To construct the loop for the bungee section, take the eight-foot section of three-eighths-inch poly rope and make a gap in it ten inches from the first end by evenly separating the braided strands of the rope. Place the three-eighths-inch fid over the first end and slip it through the gap to create a loop four inches long. Take the second end and thread it through the center of the rope two inches from the end of the first end. Pull on the second end and tighten to form a figure 8. Take the remainder of the first end and tuck it into the center of the rope. Repeat the process to make the loop on the second end. (When you make the second loop, the first loop becomes the second end.)

While you're at it, make smaller open loops (insert the fid about six inches from the end of the rope) on both ends of the quarter-inch (or three-eighths-inch)

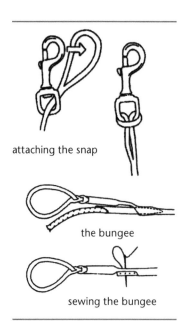

attaching the snap

the bungee

sewing the bungee

tugline section of poly rope. Loop the poly rope through the five-eighths-inch brass snap on one end of the line. Congratulations! You've just made a one-dog tugline.

Place a half-inch fid on one end of the bungee and thread the bungee into the hollow center of the three-eighths-inch poly rope about three inches from one of the loops. Securely sew the end of the bungee closest to the loop into the poly rope. Then bunch up the poly rope around the bungee, hold the bunched-up rope in place, and sew the other end of the bungee. (Bunching the poly rope is like loading the spring on a shock absorber.)

Here's an alternative way to secure the bungee: After bunching up the poly rope, bring the bungee back out so that about two and a half inches of each end of the bungee sticks out from the rope. Wrap one end of the bungee around the poly rope and bring it back next to itself. Place two hog rings around the bungee and squeeze them tight with the pliers. Repeat this with the other end of the bungee.

After the bungee is secured by either method, slip shrink wrap over each of the sewn bungee/poly rope areas and melt it with a hair dryer or *carefully* with a lighter or over a gas stove-top burner.

Putting It Together

In the bungee section of the line, the bungee cord should always be closest to your body. Take the end of the rope that is opposite the end that has the bungee in it and loop it together with the tugline section to make a one-dog skijoring line.

To make a two- or three-dog line, you can simply add extra tuglines to the loop in the bungee section. As an alternative, some line builders attach a heavy-duty O-ring or a carabiner to that end of the bungee

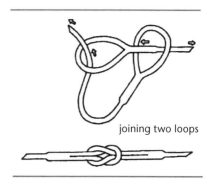

joining two loops

section to make it easier to attach multiple tuglines. If you want to skijor with a longer line, increase the length of the three-eighths-inch poly rope or use longer tuglines.

A Few Hints and Warnings

- Don't use a lightweight or plain rubber bungee cord. Make sure the bungee you use is an arctic cord and extra sturdy. The outside of an arctic bungee is often a tough black fabric. If you look at the cut end of the bungee, the rubber fibers inside should be small and densely packed. The rubber bungees with hooks at either end sometimes snap in the cold.
- If you buy or make a line in which the ends of the bungee cord are attached internally to the poly rope, rather than being looped around the outside of the rope, make sure the bungee cord is sewn in with heavy-duty thread or floss. Hog rings will not hold in this case, because they rip through the ends of the bungee cord.
- Buy good-quality Italian brass snaps. Cheap snaps won't hold up under the stress of dog driving.
- If your poly rope is frayed, melt the frayed end with a match or lighter before trying to tuck it into the fid.

Booties

Here are directions for sewing dog booties:

1. Cut a ten-inch-by-four-inch rectangle of Polar Plus fabric.
2. Cut a one-inch-by-three-and-a-half-inch strip of Velcro loop material and a one-inch-by-four-inch strip of Velcro hook material.
3. Attach the Velcro as follows:
   - Sew the loop Velcro onto the top of the rectangle, sewing all four sides down.
   - Sew one end of the hook Velcro adjacent to the loop piece, being sure to place the piece with its hooks down.

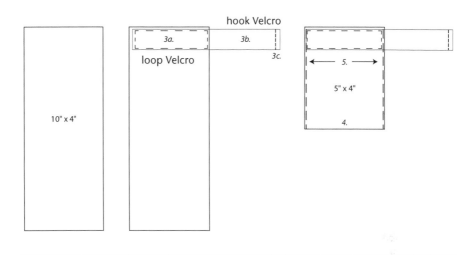

- Fold the last half inch of the hook piece back and sew the fold down. This gives you something to hold onto when releasing the Velcro and removing the bootie.
4. Fold the Polar Plus rectangle in half, being sure the Velcro is on the outside.
5. Sew both longer sides of the rectangle. (These booties are designed to be worn with the seams on the outside.)

Plan Ahead for Conditions

The type of equipment and clothing you choose for any given outing will depend on the temperature (including potential wind-chill), the snow conditions, the length of your outing, the terrain, and the comfort level you want. Dressing properly and using the right kind of ski wax can be a real challenge, particularly when conditions change while you're on the trail. Varying conditions can also affect your dog's performance.

Temperature affects not just the amount of clothing you need to put on but also the needs of your dog. In temperatures above twenty-five degrees Fahrenheit or when working in hot sunshine, your dog may become overheated. If you plan to run in warm weather, bring water for the dog and take frequent breaks to let him cool off. If at all possible, avoid overheating yourself and becoming drenched in sweat. Layer your clothing so that you can shed as you get warmer.

Conversely, low temperatures mean you need to dress carefully to stay warm and to protect your feet, hands, and face. A short-haired dog may need a dog coat in cold and windy weather. Don't forget to factor in windchill. The thermometer may read a comfortable twenty degrees Fahrenheit, but that reading will seem irrelevant if you're skiing in a twenty-mile-per-hour wind. You'll need windproof clothing from top to bottom and perhaps a face mask. Wind also causes you to dehydrate more quickly, so pack extra liquids for both yourself and your dog.

Snow conditions are affected by temperature. Snow that falls at higher temperatures tends to be both denser and wetter than snow that falls at lower temperatures. If you are skiing in wet snow and you tend to fall down a lot, you might want to wear waterproof outer gear. Wet snow will stick to the bottom of your dog's feet, and a dog with silky fur or long hair between his toes may develop snowballs. Cutting the hair between the toes or applying oil or ointment can minimize the snowballs, but you may need to put booties on the dog.

Dry snow usually will shed right off your clothes even if you are covered from head to toe after a fall. Likewise, snowballs become much less of a problem for dogs running in drier snow and cooler temperatures. But in extreme cold weather on dry, crystallized snow, the razor-sharp ice crystals may cut the pads of your dog's feet and even the webbing between the pads.

Snow conditions and air temperatures dictate what kind of wax to use on your skis. If you have waxless skis, you can avoid having to learn which wax to use when, but in general you also sacrifice speed and versatility when you use waxless skis.

Most waxes come with charts that explain what temperatures and types of snow they are designed for. Generally speaking, dry, cold snow is slower; powdery snow is the most forgiving; and wet snow can be both slick and sticky. (This rule of thumb doesn't necessarily apply at higher elevations, where changing weather conditions can quickly alter the quality of whatever snow is on the ground.) Ski shops and ski clubs sometimes hold waxing clinics, and ski shop personnel are usually happy to teach you how to wax your skis easily and efficiently.

Dogs with silky fur often are prone to getting snowballs, which are not just uncomfortable but can cause foot injuries.

If you are going on an extended trip, don't forget to pack different types of waxes—and a scraper—to handle the varying temperatures and snow conditions you are sure to encounter. If it's windy, use a wax for colder conditions than the air temperature would dictate.

If you are skijoring on groomed trails, remember that trail conditions are affected not just by the current temperature but also by the conditions under which the snow originally fell and by the type and frequency of grooming. The snow pack on a regularly maintained trail can be grainy, icy, powdery, sticky, loose, crusty, crystallized, hard, or mushy, not to mention fast or slow. On a groomed trail, wet snow will set up a little differently than dry snow. The wax you choose may be determined more by how recently the trail was groomed or by the nature of the last snowfall than by the current air temperature.

The length of your outing will dictate how carefully you should dress and whether you need to bring a change of clothes. If you plan to travel overnight, bring at least one complete change of clothing and be sure to take along appropriate gear for abrupt changes in weather. If you plan to go around the block, you can pretty much throw on whatever is handiest in the closet, within reason. But use some judgment here: it's entirely possible to get frostbite even on a three-mile run. It's also not unheard of to lose your team and be forced to ski home. A short jaunt shouldn't require any special equipment for the dog, other than booties if conditions warrant, but you might want to pack booties, snacks, and water for a longer day trip and more complete gear for overnighters.

Terrain makes a big difference in what kind of gear you should wear and bring. If you're traveling in backcountry or on trails with long hills, you'll be exerting so much at times that you'll want to wear clothing that wicks away perspiration and layers that can be shed to keep from overheating. You'll also want to bring water to keep both you and your dog well hydrated. Remember that if a trail runs along the shadow of a hill, it will be colder than one in bright sunlight. If you'll be crossing creeks or overflow, don't forget to bring a scraper to remove ice from your skis.

Comfort is a relative thing, and nowhere is that more apparent than at skijoring races. On a cold December day, you'll see everything from huge parkas and bulky snow pants to body-fitting Lycra that makes you shiver just to look at it. Some people tolerate the cold more easily than others; some people simply have less sense! If you've been frostbitten on any portion of your body, such as your nose, ears, or hands, be sure to give that part extra protection. If you're tough, go ahead and wear lightweight, thin clothing. But by all means, don't skimp if it will make you miserable.

The same goes for preparations. Some people belong to the minimalist school of thought: Do the minimum of preparation and let the details take care of themselves. There's nothing wrong with this attitude as long as the dog is taken care of (a dog can't speak up and tell you he wants to go home because his feet are sore) and the person is not endangering himself. But if you are not ultraflexible and don't enjoy being miserable, do a little advance planning and carefully examine the conditions under which you'll be skijoring.

4

Teaching Your
Dog to Skijor

Teaching a dog to skijor involves harnessing the dog's natural pulling instinct and shaping it into a lifelong love of pulling. Our approach is neither the "right" way nor the only way to train your dog. The techniques set forth in this chapter are ones we've used and found effective; you may find different methods work better for you.

Whether it's a simple "Sit!" or complicated obedience work, ask four people how to train a dog and you'll get four different answers. There are probably as many dog-training methods and philosophies as there are dog breeds. If you are a novice dog trainer, we recommend you pick up more than one book on dog training (our bibliography lists several). Even if you've worked with dogs all your life, reading a dog-training book will almost certainly turn up something new to learn—a fresh perspective or a subtle training technique you may not have thought of. In recent years, several books have addressed research into dog behavior and the new ways that we are asking dogs to work, and these are well worth reading. A deeper understanding of how your dog thinks will pay off with huge bonuses in training.

No matter how you train, building trust and communication between you and your dog should be the top priority. To create a true partnership between you and your skijoring dog, you need to be able to communicate with and understand him. You need to respect the dog as your partner. Be careful not to betray your dog's trust in you. If you're in a foul mood on a day you'd planned to train, it's better to stay home. There's no point in training if you're not capable of being both positive and patient, and it is possible to destroy your dog's trust through a single incidence of losing your temper. The risk isn't worth it.

Dogs and their trainers develop a language between them, based on a shared understanding of what certain commands mean. In *Adam's Task: Calling Animals by Name,* Vicki Hearne presents a strong case for absolute consistency in training commands and discipline. We don't agree with some of her ideas of appropriate discipline, but her discussion of language is excellent. It's impossible to summarize Hearne's philosophy in a sentence or two, but perhaps she would have forgiven this oversimplification: there cannot be true communication between dog and human if they can't agree on the meaning of the words used between them. We'll say this again later, but it bears repeating here: *Not enforcing a command is the equivalent of changing its meaning.*

Most dog trainers agree on one point: If your dog screws up, *it's always your fault.* It's true that some dogs are easier to train than others. It's also true that a personality clash between a dog and her owner can turn training into a nightmare. But the bottom line is that dogs are dogs, not people. Ultimately, your dog's behavior is your responsibility as a trainer. "I just couldn't make her do it" is no excuse unless you believe dogs are smarter than humans. (Not that we don't occasionally wonder.)

Maintaining control over your dog at all times is essential if your goal is a well-trained, hard-working, manageable dog for skijoring. A working dog must respond in a specific way to your commands to carry out a specific task. If your dog doubts your ability to control his actions, your whole training program suffers. If you own a dog but have never before done any serious training, we recommend that you and your dog take an obedience class. Although the lessons learned in obedience school are different, the training tools you will gain will help you with your training for skijoring.

We begin this chapter with a short section on teaching your pet to pull, assuming your pet already knows elementary commands such as "sit" and "stay." The section on training puppies and young adults will have several additional techniques you can use to teach your pet commands and to fine-tune your training.

One last point: We suggest you teach your dog the commonly known commands for dog driving:

- **Gee** (pronounced with a soft *g*) to turn to the right
- **Haw** to turn to the left
- **Easy** to slow down
- **Straight ahead** or **on by** to ignore distractions and/or go past a turn
- **Line out** to keep the tugline tight
- **Whoa** to stop
- **Get up** or **hike** to speed up

If you ever add an already trained dog to your team, it's going to create some interesting situations if the new dog knows "gee" but your dog knows "go right." If you ever lend or sell your dog to other skijorers or mushers, you'll want the commands they use to be consistent with what your dog knows.

How you give a particular command is important. Speed-up commands are usually given in short, high tones that often are repeated, such as "Hike! Hike! Hike!" On the other hand, "Whoa" and "Easy" are usually given as one low, continuous, drawn-out tone. High, short, and repeated tones are more stimulating to the dog; lower, soothing, single tones tend to be calming and can help slow down the dog. (Patricia McConnell's book *The Other End of the Leash* has a fascinating discussion on acoustic signals and their effects on dogs.)

Skijoring 101: Teaching Your Dog to Pull

Perhaps you've seen or heard of skijoring, and your dog always pulls you off your feet when you walk him. You can ski pretty well, you figure, so why not try letting your dog pull you legitimately? So you don a pair of skis, put a harness on the dog, grab hold of the line, and say, "Okay, Speedy, let's go!" Your dog immediately leans into the harness, the two of you are off to a smooth start, and thus begins a partnership made in heaven. Right? Well, not always.

For the beginner, the sport of being pulled on skis by a dog in harness can end up more fiasco than fun. As in learning almost anything new, advance preparation can make a big difference in your and your dog's level of enjoyment.

Your dog may react in any of several undesirable ways when you first try to skijor with him. He may be afraid of the harness or the skis. He may be reluctant to pull you. He may want to run behind you, instead of out in front. He may bolt like a scared rabbit for half a mile, then decide that walking is the pace of choice for the next two miles. Every once in a while, a dog comes along that instantly takes to skijoring as if it were the most natural thing in the world, but this is the exception, not the rule.

Patience and a step-by-step approach will make the learning process much smoother. Harness train your dog gradually. Start out by putting the harness on and letting the dog get used to the feel of it. Don't insist that he pull the first time he wears it. Take the dog for a walk with a leash or line attached to the back of his harness, but without anything (besides you) behind him. If your dog will walk in front of you, and he pulls, keep some light pressure on the line and give him lots of praise to show him it is okay to pull when he has a harness on. This will be particularly important if he is obedience-trained and is used to heeling with an obedience collar. Make sure you take off the obedience collar before training with the harness. Wearing the collar should become a cue that he should heel, and the harness a cue that he should pull.

If your dog is not yet ready to pull with you behind him, walk beside him until he seems relaxed about the harness, and then tie a tugline and a *light* drag, such as a small log, a chain broom, or a very small tire of no more than two to five pounds to the harness and walk your dog as he pulls the drag. (A chain broom is a small bundle of chains tied to a line that attaches to the dog's harness.)

DAPHNE LEWIS

Using lightweight tires such as these, you can train a dog to pull, wait, go gee or haw, and speed up or slow down. These dogs have been trained to enjoy pulling tires by going to a place called a "target," where they are allowed to play.

Whatever drag you use should be relatively light in proportion to the dog's weight, but should create enough friction so that it doesn't slide up and hit the dog. Never leave a dog unattended with a drag behind him.

This second step is particularly important if your dog is obedience-trained. You've taught him that the obedience collar means no pulling; now you need to teach him that the harness means pulling is acceptable. Keep the lessons short—fifteen minutes at a time is plenty. Once your dog is comfortable with the harness and with pulling a weight, you can gradually drop back to get him accustomed to the idea of having you behind him, instead of next to him.

When you think your dog is ready to graduate to pulling you on your skis, don't immediately go on a ten-mile run. Start with short distances and stay on the flatlands. Choose a quiet trail, preferably with soft snow and no distractions. Remember that dogs need physical conditioning as much as humans do. Keep the experience fun by stopping *before* your dog gets tired, not after. Avoid going around a trail three or four times in the same day; the dog may become bored and decide skijoring is drudgery. Last, be extremely careful not to fall on the dog or hurt or frighten him with your skis.

If your dog seems reluctant to pull, try tapping into his chase instinct. Ask a friend to skijor in front of you; better yet, have your friend skijor with your dog while you ski or skijor ahead. Chasing often works; chasing "Mom" or "Dad" (the dog's owner) almost *always* works! Once you've persuaded your dog to pull you, you can teach him the common commands for skijoring covered later in this chapter.

Any dog that weighs more than about thirty pounds is capable of pulling, but keep in mind that not all dogs are willing. Sometimes a favorite pet simply refuses to pull, even after all our suggestions have been tried. Not every dog is cut out for skijoring. If you're satisfied that you've given it your best and the situation seems hopeless, your best move may be to find a sled dog pup or a trained skijoring dog and let your pet go back to being a pet.

Skijoring 102: Training From the pup up

The easiest way to end up with the kind of skijoring dog that best fits your needs is to start with a young pup. It's often harder and takes longer to teach an older pet dog or sled dog to skijor than to teach a puppy. This is particularly true for sled dogs accustomed to being part of a bigger team. A skijoring dog often runs alone or with just one other dog, a situation that could intimidate a team dog.

You'll need to teach your skijoring dog some commands a team dog simply has no need to know. When a sled dog—or a pet dog that has missed out on a lot of basic training—is six or seven years old, it's harder to persuade him to stop on command or to wait for

The chase instinct can be a powerful motivational tool.

you while you put on your skis. When you try to stop with trained sled dogs, they tend to lean into the harness because they are used to being anchored with a snow hook.

Socializing Techniques

The earlier you can begin to mold a dog to meet your expectations, the easier all your subsequent training will be. If you have a litter of pups at home, it's important to begin socializing them from the time they are two weeks old. Even before their eyes open, they can feel your touch. They will quickly become accustomed to your voice as soon as they can hear. Socialization during the first few weeks of a dog's life has far-reaching effects on its overall development.

When the pups get a little older, it's helpful to have kids around to play with the pups and socialize them. If you don't have kids, make sure to play with the pup yourself. Pick up her feet and get her used to being handled while it's still easy to do. If the pup becomes shy about being handled, later on you will find it much harder to groom her, cut toenails, or treat injuries. It takes much more time to work on a dog that is stiff as a board or trying frantically to get away from you than it takes to work on a dog that is relaxed and knows everything will be just fine. If you've worked with a dog since puppyhood, you'll have no trouble cutting nails or putting ointment on a sore foot even when the dog reaches fifty pounds or more.

How your dog is socialized during the first year is crucial. After that first year, if the dog has just been sitting on a chain and all of a sudden you expose him to crowds and strange noises, you will have a hard time getting the dog to respond appropriately. It's similar to a child who never sees other kids until he's old enough for school. Then suddenly he's supposed to be socialized and know how to share, but how is he expected to know about these things?

Take the pup out and socialize him with other people. The more places, people, and unthreatening situations you expose your young dog to, the better off he will be. Later on, when you begin skijoring, you'll know what to expect from your dog under all kinds of conditions. If someday you'll be racing past crowds of people, you'll know it won't bother your dog because he has been around lots of people before and knows he can trust you.

When pups reach eight to ten weeks of age, they become curious. If you can, take your pup on walks, perhaps on the trails you will later skijor. Teach the dog to follow you, or even better, to run in front of you but always to come back to you when you call. You can also teach her to lie down and stay while you walk down the trail a little bit, and then call her to you. Use positive reinforcement and play-training (training designed to be fun for the dog) so your puppy doesn't decide training is drudgery. Teaching basic commands now will come in handy later on. If someday you lose your dog while skijoring, you'll be able to tell her to come back to you or to lie down and wait till you get up to her.

Expose your pup to as many different types of terrain as possible. Take her over rocky trails, on ice (if you have any), on cement, up ramps and stairs, through water, through tunnels, over logs. Your goal is to develop the pup's confidence no matter what is underfoot. If you have a fenced yard for your pup, stock it with a variety of objects—perhaps a wooden spool, a culvert or tunnel, steps, big tires, platforms, ramps—and encourage your pup to play on and around them. The more your pup is exposed to at an early age, the better she will respond to challenges later on.

Obedience Work Versus Harness Training

Basic obedience commands such as "sit," "stay," and "lie down" can be taught to pups during their first three or four months, as can leash training. "Stand" (or "stay") is a particularly good command to teach as part of the early training process. Those who hunt with dogs frequently use this command, and it is extremely useful when the dog has to wait for the "go" command when starting out skijoring. A simple way to teach a dog to stand or stay is to use the top of a doghouse, a small training table, or just a piece of plywood on the ground. Place the pup on the table or plywood and give the command "Stand." Every time he tries to get off, put him back on, give him the command again, and tell him "good dog." Pet his back in a gentle, calming manner while teaching this, so that the command has a positive association. This command should be reinforced during leash and harness training. There are few experiences more frustrating to a skijorer than trying to get back up from a fall when your dog refuses to stay and keeps pulling you off your feet.

As a corollary to this command, Carol teaches her dogs the command "On your house." She finds it much easier to cut toenails, comb out shedding coats, examine feet for injuries, or give vaccinations and medication when the dog is on top of a doghouse. It also helps to forestall jumping on visitors.

DAVE PARTEE

This fast and powerful skijoring dog has been asked to stand still for a photo shoot. Obedience training and training to pull are by no means incompatible.

Once your pup is about five months old, you can begin more focused training. Many people have asked us, "If you are going to do both obedience training and harness training, should you do both at once or one first and then the other?" You should be able to do both at once because you are using two different tools: the collar and the harness. Most dogs quickly come to understand that pressure on the harness means "pull" and pressure on the collar means "don't pull." Some dogs, however, aren't quite sharp enough to comprehend the difference between the two. Watch how the individual dog responds to initial training. If he doesn't get the point, tackle one thing at a time. If you need to choose between the two types of training, do obedience work first because it includes many commands and behaviors you'll need for skijoring.

If you have high ambitions for your dog, obedience training is a challenging task that can keep you busy for your dog's first year. You may be burning to compete in skijoring races with your new dog, but be careful not to ask for too much before she is ready. Mari has seen cases where a dog driver, eager to race a yearling during its first season, pushed the dog too early and burned it out as a result. A young dog may pull well the first year but then do poorly the second year because she gave it all too soon. In most cases, a pup's or yearling's "all" is too much to ask. To avoid damaging a good dog, examine each situation individually and read your dog carefully. If you seem to be pushing your dog, slow down. Working with animals requires you to be a bit of a psychologist because each dog is different. Even in an open-class (unlimited) sled-dog team, each dog is an individual. You have to know what each dog can or cannot do, no matter the size of your team.

Even if you decide to forgo obedience work, we suggest you read a few books on the subject and choose a particular training philosophy to follow. Your training methods will be more effective if they are consistent and logical. Many dog-training books also suggest humane and effective disciplining techniques. Deciding ahead of time which kind of correction you wish to use for which kind of transgression will make it easier to respond appropriately when the situation arises.

Harness Training

Sled dogs usually can be harness trained at around five months old, but some mature later than others. Although dog drivers commonly speak of "breaking" a dog to harness, this is a misnomer—it's not a question of forcing the dog to pull or in any way breaking its spirit. Pulling should be fun, not frightening. If the dog is not ready to be harness broken, wait a couple of weeks. Realize, too, that males can be a little slower to mature than females.

The easiest way to harness train a pup is to hitch up a sled-dog team with your pup and several steady adults. The pup will learn much more quickly from other dogs than from you. But if you don't have other dogs to show your pup how it's done, you have to become the primary teacher. Training without the help of a veteran dog or two will take a little longer, but it can also foster a closer bond between you and your dog.

DAVE PARTEE

Skijoring is a rewards-based activity. Most dogs are ecstatic to be allowed to pull as hard as they want and run as fast as they want, especially when you come along with them.

To begin the harness-training process, put a small harness on the pup and walk him on a leash. Before you put any weight behind him, let him get used to the feel of the harness itself. *Never leave a harness on an unsupervised puppy.* A dog can destroy a harness literally in seconds, and puppies in particular are likely to react to the strange feeling of the harness by chewing on it. If your dog actually eats a harness, which dogs have been known to do, you may end up with a hefty vet bill or even a dead dog.

Once your pup seems comfortable with the harness, tie a very light drag behind the harness. Use something that moves easily over the ground and isn't hard to pull, such as a small log, a chain broom, or a small, light tire. Give him a start-up command such as "Let's go!" or "Hike!" Some dog drivers use the word "Okay," but be forewarned: It's easy to use the word in casual conversation, and saying "Okay" accidentally is a great way to have your arm pulled out of its socket or to watch your dogs take off without you.

Some dogs require more encouragement than others. Give your start-up command in a lighthearted, excited tone of voice, so your good humor will carry over to the dog. Make this pulling business sound like fun for the pup, and be liberal with your praise when he pulls. If he seems reluctant to move forward, reinforce the command by putting your hand behind the base of his tail or on the back of his thigh and gently nudging him forward. Walk forward yourself at the same time to give him extra confidence. If the drag offers too much resistance, switch to a lighter drag.

Be sure to use the command "Whoa" whenever you want the pup to stop, so that he learns to stop when you tell him to, not when he wants to. Discourage him from running back to you when you stop; instead, teach him to stand still after stopping. Although this training should be fun, the dog should also understand that he is obeying commands. In obedience training, when you use the obedience collar, the dog understands that the collar means you are going to be doing obedience work. The same principle is at work when you harness train. When you put the harness on your pup, he should learn that he is expected to pull. It shouldn't be drudgery, but the dog should clearly understand the distinction between playing and pulling.

Keep these sessions short and make sure you always end your training on a positive note, when the dog is still pulling hard. If you don't let him become discouraged, and he doesn't learn that he can get away with not pulling, he will be much less likely to slack off or become sour later on.

At the same time that your pup begins to pull, he should learn to ignore distractions. Every time he tries to go off the trail to check out an interesting diversion, give him the command "straight ahead" or "on by," and make sure he obeys. At this point, you will probably want to walk him on a leash while he pulls, so that you can easily reinforce the command.

This part of harness training can be hard for a puppy to understand. It's vitally important to keep it fun, and all the more so if the pup has no older dog to watch, no seasoned puller to keep him on the path. A well-mannered adult dog will usually teach the pup that he is supposed to pull straight down the trail and go by everything else, but if you don't have that luxury, you need to be firm and consistent with your teaching. You have to teach the dog not to go off in the trees and not to stop whenever he wants to. Keep the lessons upbeat and, as we said before, be lavish in your praise.

As the pup begins to pull more steadily, you can increase the weight of the drag a little. Be careful to avoid anything too heavy until the dog is at least six months old, or you may damage his muscle tone and bone structure, which is still soft. Some of the larger breeds should not pull any significant weight until they are at least a year old.

Graduating to Skis

When the pup is pulling well, switch to having her pull you instead of a drag. Walk or run behind her, keeping a constant pressure on the line. Wait until the pup is comfortable with both the feel of the harness and the idea of pulling you before you start skiing behind her. Also, be sure the dog is big enough to pull your weight comfortably. This will depend on the individual dog's weight, size, and attitude, but pulling a person usually isn't undertaken until the dog is at least six months old. It's much more difficult for a single dog to pull you than for two dogs to take on more than twice your weight—the synergism between two or more dogs can be astounding—and for a still-developing pup, pulling you is even more difficult. However, you can ski with the dog loose at first, which will introduce her to the skis and give her the idea that they mean you'll both go off and have fun.

HOWLING DOG ALASKA

This puppy is learning to pull and to stay out in front by working alongside his mother. His trainer begins step by step—walking the puppy while he pulls in harness, then graduating to the faster pace of skiing, biking, or scootering.

When the dog is big enough and you've skied with her loose at least once or twice to get her used to your skis, it's time to put the harness on, hitch up the dog, and try to persuade her to pull you on skis for five minutes or so. If she doesn't catch on right away, take off the line and try again a little later. Be upbeat about the whole thing. Try to convey to the dog that this is the life; this is what she was born to do.

When you begin training on trails, start out when there's new snow so your skis don't make much noise. Choose flat trails that make the dog feel that she's actually pulling, not just running ahead of you. You may want to leave your poles behind for the first few sessions. Don't go very far at first. Keep the training periods brief (fifteen to twenty minutes) and the distance short (one to three miles). You can help the dog by skating or double poling, but be careful not to scare the dog. Don't fall on your dog or strike her with your skis or poles. It's vitally important that she learn to trust both you and the skis. If she doesn't trust the skis, you will have a major problem on your hands.

Skijoring Command Basics

Even before your dog has learned to pull, you can start teaching him a few new commands. Remember to teach one command at a time, progressing to the next command only after the dog has mastered the one before it. Be sure to maintain full control at all times. Don't give a command when you can't correct the dog if he does the wrong thing. Be sure your dog understands the command "no" or "wrong" so that you can give him right-versus-wrong cues as he's learning.

By now your dog should already know how to sit, stand, stay, lie down, and come, as well as the commands "let's go," "straight ahead" or "on by," and "whoa." The next step is to teach him "easy," "gee," "haw," "line out," and possibly "come around." You don't have to wait for snow to teach these commands; in fact, they are easier to teach on foot during the summer. (You can also teach these commands out of the order given here, by the way.) You can train the dog on a leash or in harness with you behind her. If you train on a leash, train for no more than fifteen minutes at a time.

Easy

The command "easy" is used to slow down the pace without actually stopping. This command comes in handy in situations when you need to reduce either speed or power, such as when negotiating rough trails, taking tight or blind turns, going down hills, crossing roads, or skijoring behind another team. It can also be used to regulate your dog's speed when you need to conserve her strength on a long run.

To practice this, harness up your dog and run behind her, holding a line attached to the harness. In a slow, calm tone, say "easy" and at the same time pull back on the line until the dog slows down to a trot or a walk. Say the word in a way that supports the command: long, low, and drawn out. Make the command clear by holding the dog to a slow pace for about a minute. Then let up on the rope and encourage her to pick up speed again. You can teach this command on skis, but you need to be good at snowplowing so you can effectively slow the dog down to reinforce the command.

Some dog drivers teach the command "walk" to tell their dogs to move forward without pulling at all. This command can be handy for maneuvering a team to the start line or moving through a crowd at a trailhead. It is also a useful alternative to the command "heel" for teaching a pulling dog to behave on a leash.

Gee and Haw

Gee-haw training can require a lot of patience. Some dogs seem to take forever to learn these commands; others pick it up in just a few sessions. And then there's one of Carol's leaders, Rissa, who picked up the "gee" command when she was just a yearling. Yet for the rest of her life she was still valiantly trying to understand what "haw" meant.

This may seem like stating the obvious, but you should know gee (right) and haw (left) yourself before you begin teaching your pup. A good friend of ours, Lynn Orbison, habitually mixed up these two commands. Sometimes Lynn's long-suffering golden retriever, Shawna, would look back to see in which direction Lynn was pointing. Other times she'd go exactly where Lynn had told her to go, for which Lynn would berate her. Lynn was invariably embarrassed, because Shawna was usually correct. (Luckily, Shawna always forgave her.) If you have problems keeping the two commands straight, you might want to make mittens with the words *gee* and *haw* on them or wear a certain ring on one hand.

Summer is a good time to work on directional commands. You can either walk your dog on a leash or wear your skijoring belt and harness up the dog using your skijoring line. Work on one direction at a time. As you approach an intersection, say the dog's name and then "gee." At the same time, walk over to the right so the dog can see you. Pull the dog into the right-hand turn and repeat the command a few times as you do so.

After the dog goes in the correct direction, give him lots of praise. If he doesn't turn correctly, walk back about a hundred feet and try again. If the dog still doesn't understand the command after three to five times, stop the training and try the exercise again the next day. Be sure to vary your training runs, so that the dog doesn't simply memorize which direction to take at a particular intersection.

Give the directional command just before the turn, not one hundred feet before it or halfway into it. Giving the command before the dog can even see the intersection is pointless; likewise, giving the command in the middle of the intersection gives the dog no time at all to process the situation. In Miki and Julie Collins's book *Dog Driver: A Guide for the Serious Musher,* they suggest you watch your dog as you approach an intersection. Often the dog will lift his head and perk his ears when he realizes a decision is forthcoming. That's your signal to give the command.

Dogs seem to be just like people in that some know which way to turn in an instant, while others need a moment to remember which way is which. Carol has found that for dogs who don't think quite as fast, a gentle warning (okay, we're going to go "gee" up here) works wonders. She owned an excellent gee-haw lead dog named Iris who would happily take any turn you asked her to take, provided you gave her a moment to figure it out. Mari always says "easy" as a cue before she gets to a turn to alert the dogs of a forthcoming directional command.

If you have an already-trained leader that knows gee and haw, often you can use that dog to help train your pup. But be sure your pup actually learns the commands. Many an apparent gee-haw leader has turned out to be something less when taken away from his partner. Rissa never missed a single turn when she ran next to Carol's old veteran, Shiner. But when she ran alone, it became obvious that she'd been taking cues off Shiner rather than learning the commands for herself. The only way to verify that your dog has truly learned gee and haw is to run him by himself or next to a dog that doesn't know the commands at all.

If you have an adult dog that doesn't know gee and haw, it's better to train the pup alone. Because the other dog doesn't know what he's doing, he may teach the pup bad manners or confuse the pup with the wrong response.

Line Out

When a dog is given the command to "line out," she should lean forward in the harness and keep her tugline tight. Some skijorers don't bother teaching their dogs this command, particularly if they run only one dog or their dogs are calm and well mannered when starting out. But if you are skijoring with more than one dog or are training puppies, or if your dogs are unruly enough to cause you problems, the "line out" command may be an important one to teach.

To teach this command, harness up your dog and put on your skijoring belt. Go for a short walk or run, give the "whoa" command, and wait for the dog to come to a halt, keeping slight tension on the line. Then give the command to line out, keeping gentle backward pressure on the line.

If the dog doesn't remain lined out and pointing forward, reinforce the command by going up to her and placing her back in the correct position, maintaining gentle backward pressure on the tugline as much as possible. It's easier to enforce this command if your dog also will stay on command. If she knows "stay," use that to convey to her that she is supposed to stay in that position. If you train with a friend, have your friend reinforce the command from the front while you maintain tension on the line from the

DAVE PARTEE

These dogs are lined out and ready to launch off the starting line. The driver is kneeling to maintain control.

back. You can also reinforce the command by anchoring the dog to a post or tree and walking out in front of her. Be patient: this command sometimes takes a while to make sense to a dog.

For some dogs, the impulse to come back to you when they are confused makes it very difficult to teach them to line out. You can make a training tool for this purpose by setting up a platform and a post in front of it, with a line going from the dog's collar forward to the post and back to you. That way, you can reinforce the command by a gentle tug of the line while standing behind the dog.

Come Around

Some dog drivers believe it is a bad idea to teach a dog to turn around and come back to you on command. The idea is that this teaches the dog the bad habit of quitting or heading for home. A great deal depends on the dog's level of intelligence, on the amount of training you've done with him, and on your level of control. Carol successfully taught her first skijoring dog to come around on command without any of the problems others have had. However, if you do teach your dog to come around, be sure that you teach him to do so only on command. Teaching the dog to line out will help counteract any tendencies to come around on his own. If the dog has the "whoa" or "stay" command down, you will have a way to tell him to stop if you don't want him to come around right then.

More Skijoring Techniques
Tackling Hills

After you and your dog have been skijoring together and have mastered the flatlands, you can begin to teach your dog how to pull you up hills. The guiding principle is this: When you come to an incline, *never stop on the hill.* If you quit, you have taught your dog a bad habit by example. From that time on, she may habitually remember to quit on the hill. So you have to think, "Okay, I'm going to make it up this hill," and encourage the dog to do the same. You have to help the dog, too. Don't make it hard on her by hanging back there like a sack of potatoes. This means you have to be in fairly good shape yourself.

Get a good running start and charge up the hill as steadily as you can. If the dog acts as if she wants to stop, keep her going to the top of the hill and a little farther, and then stop and praise her. You might even give her a little snack if you think she needs extra reinforcement. When you stop after climbing a hill, don't stop at the same place every time, or the dog will learn to stop at that specific point in the trail. As the dog gets in better and better shape, you can ask her to go a little farther past the hill every time.

An aside about snacks: It's acceptable to occasionally give snacks after going around a trail or up a steep hill, but the habit can be overdone. If you make it a too-regular habit to stop after a steep hill and give your dog a snack, you are likely to find your dog stopping after *every* steep hill, waiting for that reward. Generally, you don't want to snack your dog in the middle of a short run. Afterward is fine, and it's good to give a recovery treat if your dog has been working hard.

When you teach a dog to go downhill, the dog should already know the command "easy." When you ski down a hill, snowplow to increase your control and to make the dog feel as if she's still pulling. Constantly monitor your speed so you don't run into the dog. If you can't avoid catching up, steer to the side to avoid clipping the dog with your ski tips. It may also benefit you to teach the dog the command "behind." On a steep downhill run, sometimes your dog will have to move behind you to keep from being run over. "Behind" is best taught on foot, before you ski in the hills. Some obedience training can come in handy in this situation, because "behind" can be taught in conjunction with "heel."

When going down a steep hill, it's a good idea to detach your line from your belt and hold it in your hand, so you can let go if you or your dog has a problem. If you do have to release your dog, it's important that the dog know how to lie down and stay or to come on command.

Training Around Other Dogs

Skijoring is, by nature, a solitary sport. Most of your training probably will be done alone. Because of this, your dog may react inappropriately when first confronted with company on the trail. If you eventually plan to race or train around dogs, people, and other distractions, thorough socialization is vital. Your dog should be used to seeing different things, should know not to chase after loose dogs or other distractions, and should know the command "straight ahead." Whenever he becomes distracted by something, you should correct that behavior right away. The dog should learn that he is expected to work when he is in harness and that playing or visiting is not allowed.

It's best not to allow your dog to go up to other skijoring teams uninvited. Even at informal meets and clinics ask first before assuming another driver or dog will welcome the visit.

If you've taken your dog everywhere with you, you will be far ahead. Obedience classes also are excellent training because your dog learns to walk past food, other dogs, and anything else in his way. The dog learns to listen only to you. He also learns that there is a distinction between work and play, that until he is released by your voice, he must listen and pay attention instead of fooling around.

Training More Than One Dog

If you plan to train two novice skijoring dogs, train them separately at first and then put them together so that they don't reinforce any wrong behaviors in each other while they are still learning. Normally we don't recommend training with more than two dogs because you won't have enough control. Even when Mari races in the three-dog skijoring class, she trains with only two dogs at a time. With extremely well-trained or mellow dogs, you can safely run more than two, but if you can't control them, you will lose a lot of ground in your training (not to mention endangering yourself).

If you trust your skijoring ability (and won't spook someone else's dog), borrowing a veteran skijoring dog can be an easy way to help train your novice. Sometimes a dog will learn to keep pulling steadily by running with another dog; but if you try this, make sure the second dog is well behaved. Dogs will quickly pick up behaviors from other dogs—both bad and good.

When running two dogs together, some people like to run one in front of the other, particularly on narrow trails. With that configuration, however, you sacrifice some control when passing other teams. If you run the dogs side by side, you will need to decide whether or not to neckline them together. Many skijorers run their dogs without necklines to minimize tangles. Any kind of tangle is a headache for a skijorer, but neckline tangles are a nightmare. The driver must ski up to the dogs, hoping they'll stay still, and stay balanced while untangling the lines. However, a neckline is sometimes necessary to keep a reluctant dog moving forward or to keep a wayward dog on the trail. If you do use necklines, obedient dogs that stand on command will make your life much easier if you have a tangle.

Dogs often learn to extricate themselves from tangles without any help and will free themselves if given a moment to do so. Unfortunately, some dogs take this talent a step further and learn to extricate themselves from their harnesses. If your dog happens

DAVE PARTEE

This two-dog team is running in an in-line hitch. The second dog is hooked up behind the leader rather than next to it.

to learn the bad habit of backing out of her harness, she will find it more difficult to do so if she is anchored to the other dog by a neckline. You might also want to put a belly band under the harness so the dog can't back out of it. A neckline run under the dog's stomach and clipped to the side straps of the harness works in a pinch. (It's not good for dogs to learn to back out of a harness. They never forget!)

If one dog is more of a leader than the other, you can lengthen that dog's tugline so that her head is about a neckline's length ahead of the other dog's head. An aggressive dog may overwhelm the dog next to her even without any actual physical aggression taking place. Both Mari and Carol have seen a normally good lead dog flatly refuse to run next to an aggressive dog, even though the other dog did nothing overt. If you have no choice but to run a meek leader with an aggressive leader, try lengthening the meeker dog's tugline to put her a little ahead of the aggressive one.

If you have a dog that likes to run alone, you can put that dog a little ahead of or a little behind the other dog to make her feel as if she's alone. If you have a dog that does not like to run up front, you can sometimes trick him to run lead by shortening his tugline so that he is running a head behind the other dog, but still use a neckline between them. You can also hook up the dogs in a line instead of next to each other.

To run three dogs, you can either hook them up fan-style (three abreast) or tandem-style (two side by side and one alone). When running three abreast, you can either neckline all three dogs together, neckline two of the three, or omit the necklines altogether. Whether running tandem-style or fan-style, it's important that the lead dog or dogs know how to pass and be passed.

Passing

Teaching your dog to pass other dogs can be a real challenge. Dogs are social animals by nature, and their instinct is to stop and acknowledge other dogs. To counteract this behavior, you need to

DAVE PARTEE

Three dogs in a tandem hitch.

be firm. You must convey to your dog that when you pass another team, he is not allowed to stop and sniff the other dogs. Any dog can learn this, but it's a lot easier if you start early and consistently reinforce the lesson. It's also better public relations for the whole sport of skijoring if you can avoid causing problems when you are passing or being passed. If you're training on trails used by other dog drivers, you want to be respected on that trail rather than having people say, "Oh no, here comes another skijorer!"

Before you teach your dog how to pass, he should already know the command "straight ahead" or "on by" and should obey it in all sorts of situations. You can teach this command anytime, whether you're walking, biking, skiing, or whatever. Every time the dog has to pass something—a car, another hiker, a kid, another dog—say "on by!" and make the dog ignore the distraction. When he does so, give him lots of praise. Teach him to listen just to your voice. It's best if the dog knows the command before you start skijoring with him, because it's so much harder to stop and correct the dog when you're on skis.

Even if your dog is practiced at ignoring distractions, it can be difficult to teach him to pass other teams without hesitating or refusing to run in front of the passed team. Your task is easier if you have a leader that already knows how to do it. If you don't have such a leader, find a friend with a dog to help you. You and your friend can be skiing, running, or walking with your dogs. Come up behind the other person, give the command "on by," and go past with your dog. If you are on skis, snowplow ahead of time to reduce your speed and make it easier to pass. For more control, pull up on the skijoring line (holding it at a point forward of the bungee section) so that you are closer to your dog and can help direct the dog's course or react quickly if need be.

DAVE PARTEE

Passing is an important skill to teach the skijoring dog. Practicing with small distractions and then graduating to more complicated passes with friends will prepare you and your dog for the surprise meeting with a stranger on a new trail.

As you go by, return to parallel skiing and gradually feed the line back out. Some dogs naturally keep going after a pass. Other dogs will try to slow down or stop. Encourage the dog to keep going, particularly if he begins to falter once he's out front. Have your friend stop and wait to give you time to move out ahead so your dog isn't distracted by something following closely behind him. If the dog passes correctly, give him lots of praise. It might even be beneficial to give him a snack a little ways down the trail but don't stop too soon after the pass.

After several sessions in which your friend holds back, you can work up to having your friend follow you, so that your dog learns to keep going even when something follows close behind him. It's important to practice this type of training on trails the dog is familiar with, so he doesn't have to worry about where he's going while he's learning to pass. Make sure the dog is in shape. Practice passing when the dog is well rested, at the beginning of a run instead of at the end, so the dog will want to go by and keep going. A tired dog usually will be less interested in passing and going on unless he knows he's near the end of the trail.

As with any other command, it's easier to train a novice dog to pass other teams if you have an experienced dog to show him how. Starting with two inexperienced dogs can be disastrous, and running a novice with a dog that has bad passing habits will only teach the novice those same bad habits. If you do have another dog that passes well, this is a good time to run the two with a neckline. The experienced dog can pull the novice past the other team, and the new dog will get the idea more quickly than if you try to teach him yourself. When you practice passing this way a few times, the new dog will learn that you simply don't stop. Developing this good habit early on makes future passing a lot easier.

Don't forget to teach your dog good manners when *being* passed. Train the dog to stand quietly while another team goes by. Don't allow your dog to lunge at or interfere with the passing team.

Passing is an important part of trail etiquette. Common courtesy and consideration of the other team are essential.

If you meet a dog team head-on, what should you do? There has been much debate over whether skijorers should pass dog teams on the fly or pull off the trail and reel in the dog. There's no right answer. It depends on your dog, the musher's dogs, the width of the trail, your skiing ability, and other factors. If you are a good skier, you have practiced head-on passes, and you are confident the musher's team is well trained, passing on the fly is preferable. But if you are not confident of the behavior of either your dog or the musher's dog team, the safest course of action is to pull yourself and your dog well off the trail. Be sure to pull in your ski poles as well, and if possible, place yourself between your dog and the passing team. Do not allow your dog to lunge at the passing team.

Avoiding Tangles

Many skijorers dislike necklines because of their tangle potential, particularly when passing another team. But even without necklines, accidents can happen. Mari was skijoring with two dogs on a wide ski trail with lots of ups and downs. She had come around a turn and down a hill when suddenly there was a skier directly in front of her. It was too late to stop. The dogs weren't necklined, and they passed on either side of the skier. The poor skier got caught in the skijoring line and went for quite a ride.

If you have to pass a team (or a skier), pull up on the line so you are close behind your dogs. There's no hard-and-fast rule for which side to pass on, so be ready to pass on *either* side, depending on what the other team does. Try to give a wide berth to the team you're passing. The other skier might throw out a pole, or a dog might move over toward your team. If you are being passed, pull your dogs way over to one side of the trail and make sure the other person can go by without running into your team. Not all dog drivers teach good passing manners to their dogs, so it's safer to assume the worst and leave yourself plenty of room whenever you are forced into proximity with another team.

If you skijor with a long line, maintain constant tension on it so it can't drop and become tangled in your ski tips. When you are hooking up your team, pay attention to the dogs so they don't tie knots in their lines while your head is turned.

Getting Out of Tangles

Sooner or later, you'll end up with a tangle you couldn't avoid. Some are easy to fix; some can be amazingly complicated. If your tuglines, main line, and necklines are all different colors, it's easier to visually sort out a bad tangle. That way you can see right away which line you are working with. If you are running with necklines, undo them first and see if that helps. Being able to undo tangles becomes easier with experience.

If your dog has the line wrapped around her leg or some other part of her body, it may be easier to unsnap the line than to try to

DAVE PARTEE

extricate the dog's paw or body. Be careful not to release the dog altogether! On rare occasions, a dog will get so tangled in her harness that you'll have to take it almost all the way off, but don't pull the harness over the dog's neck if you can avoid doing so.

When you have a bad tangle, stay calm. Talk quietly and reassuringly to the dogs. This is crucial. They will instantly pick up on it if you become agitated or angry and may shy away from you or refuse to stay still. Also, remember that dogs may panic in a bad tangle, particularly if a tangled line is causing them pain. Be careful: Any panicked dog may bite out of fear, even one you've raised yourself from a pup. Occasionally, tangles will precipitate a dogfight.

Whenever Carol has a bad tangle, she begins talking to the dogs before she even reaches them. She uses low, calm tones and tries to convey with her voice that the tangle is no big deal. This is especially important if you are tangled with another team and are working with dogs that don't know you. They will respond to the tone of your voice even if you are a stranger.

It's not a bad idea to carry something with you for cutting the lines in a severe tangle or for the rare instance where a tangled dog

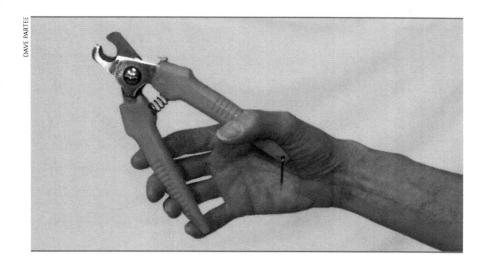

DAVE PARTEE

is in so much pain that she won't let you get near her. Mari always carries heavy-duty dog toenail clippers in her pocket. They will cut through nearly anything, even a cable gangline, and they are much safer than a knife. But the best prevention is to take out no more than two dogs at a time, and certainly no more dogs than you can easily control.

Starting Out With a Fresh Team

If your dogs are excited when you start out, hooking them up and putting on your skis can become a major operation unless you can anchor your team to something immovable. Even if your dog knows how to lie down and wait for you, anchoring your skijoring line to a stationary object may come in handy in unexpected situations. You can do this by using a separate anchoring line, also known as a snub line, attached to a tree, post, car, or other immovable object. Attach a quick-release snap to the end of the line and clip the anchored quick release to your skijoring line at the ring or loop where the tuglines attach to the main (bungee cord) line. That way, the anchor will be positioned ahead of the bungee. When your skis are on and you are ready to go, hook the skijoring line into your belt, pull back on the quick release, and off you go— leaving the quick-release snap and anchoring line behind.

Hassles and frustrations at the beginning of a run will often set the tone for the entire run. Most problems seem to happen in the first two hundred to three hundred yards. The dogs normally calm down after that. Everything you can do to guarantee a smooth start will help you past that initial hump.

Starting Out at a Trailhead

If you train away from home, you'll need a way to tie out your dogs once you arrive at the trail. Some people use a cable picket, which is a length of cable with short sections attached at intervals for each individual dog. Unfortunately, some dogs get easily tangled in a picket cable, and the cable also requires a stationary post at

SARA ELZEY

Transporting ten dogs in a Jeep is challenging enough; finding places to tie them all requires additional creativity.

each end to tie off to. Many dog drivers put eyebolts around the lower frame of their vehicles and use short lengths of chain, called "drop chains," to quickly and safely anchor each dog to the vehicle.

Potential Problems and Possible Solutions

The average dog takes to skijoring with time and proper training. But problems do occasionally arise. A training or behavioral problem can be overcome by analyzing its cause and planning a strategy for its resolution. Patience and consistency will usually bring around a problem dog.

Dogs That Don't Pull

Some dogs have a difficult time comprehending what's expected of them when they're in harness. Walking beside the dog as he pulls a drag can help get the message across. This also is a great way to practice before snow or to teach young dogs how to pull. For the

MONA LURÅS

drag, you can make a "chain broom"—a bundle of chain lengths tied to a line that goes to the back of the dog's harness. Add or remove chain lengths to control the weight. For young dogs, the weight should be light, just enough to teach them to pull against resistance. For older dogs, you can use a chain broom for strength training. But *always* have the dog on a leash when you do this, and work on a quiet, smooth surface so the noise of the chains doesn't frighten the dog and the links can't get caught on small brush or other obstacles. (Check out the article by Mona Lurås in the August/September 2009 issue of *Dog & Driver* for more information.)

As we've said before, chasing can be helpful in training a dog to pull. During our clinics, we've often watched as beginners skijored behind an experienced person and the novice dogs quickly picked up on what was expected of them. It's important, however, not to follow other teams too closely or to chase another team every time you go out. Otherwise, after a while the dog won't want to go by himself—he'll become too dependent on chasing. Skijoring requires the dog to be a leader. On the other hand, a skijoring leader is under less pressure than a dog-team leader that might have ten other dogs behind him. A skijoring dog doesn't necessarily have to be capable of running alone or in front of another dog. Carol's dog Dodger was a good example. Dodger would not run lead even in a three-dog team because he became nervous if another dog was running behind him. Nor did he pull consistently if he ran alone. But he pulled quite well as long as he had another experienced dog next to him.

In a slightly different case, Carol tried skijoring with Neelix, a thirteen-year-old veteran sled dog that often ran lead. When she said, "Let's go!" he walked sedately in front of her, his tugline slack. She added an even older veteran, fourteen-year-old Ranger, that loved to go out but no longer pulled. With Ranger beside him, Neelix immediately dug in. He was perfectly happy to do all the work; he just needed some company.

Mari has had several great leaders that simply refused to run by themselves in front of a skijorer. She also has had some exceptional leaders that would do anything—from the one-dog junior sled class (which asks a lot of a dog) to running lead in open-class sled-dog races (where the number of dogs in a team is unlimited) to being a great skijor dog. It comes down to the dog having a *lot* of confidence and trust in you, and to great teamwork.

Insecure or Shy Dogs

Modifying the behavior of an insecure dog is easiest when the dog is young, but even older dogs that are shy can be brought around. Take the dog everywhere with you, so that she learns to trust both you and other people. Sometimes an insecure dog simply needs attention, and often that extra attention pays off in intense loyalty. The dog will do anything for you because she has learned to trust you.

Correcting an insecure dog can be a tricky proposition. The dog needs to understand the word "no," but a too-stern "no!" may be enough to make her drop to the ground or urinate submissively. You will need to figure out how to use the word calmly yet firmly, without frightening the dog. Know each dog as an individual, so that you know how to communicate displeasure or an incorrect choice. Insecure dogs require a gentle hand and careful, low-key verbal correction.

Direct eye contact is a form of dominance; if you hold a dog by the neck and look her in the eye, and she boldly stares back, you have a problem! When Mari trained Scott, one of her particularly tough border collies, she would sometimes place him on his back, crouch over him, and stare him right in the eye. Using that technique on her more soft-headed border collie Bess would have sent Bess running off to the neighbors. If your goal is to be a competent dog handler, it's important to read and treat each dog as an individual.

A shy skijoring dog can pose major problems. You need to be able to handle the dog, and some dogs are so shy that they spook at a mere touch. Again, socialization is important. Skijoring can be even more frightening than Alaska-style dog mushing, and a shy or insecure dog may become so frightened that she refuses ever to run in front of skis. But bringing around a shy dog and watching her gain confidence can be a tremendously rewarding endeavor.

Ski-Shy Dogs

Dogs exposed to skis at an early age tend to be less leery of them than dogs introduced to skis later in life. Some dogs are immediately distrustful of those funny sticks on your feet. Others start out unafraid but become spooked because they've been hurt or frightened by the skis. Once a dog develops a fear of skis, it may take a lot to alleviate that fear, so it's important not to injure or frighten your dog with your skis. Never start out harness breaking your dog on ice or noisy snow. Wait for a day when it has just snowed and the trail is soft and quiet. Also, get your dog used to running or walking in front of you with his harness and skijor line attached to you before you introduce the skis.

If you do have a ski-shy dog, it may take time and lots of patience to bring him around. To build his confidence, skijor on flat, quiet trails where the skis don't make noise and you have little to no risk of falling. Even if you work him out of his fear once, there is the potential that he will become afraid of the skis again. This is a problem you should try to avoid at all costs.

If your dog refuses to pull in front of skis at all, try to desensitize him by carrying the skis with you whenever you are in your dog's yard, or by leaving them on the ground near him. If you can do so, let him run loose while you ski so he begins to associate skis with positive experiences. If he's spooked but will still pull, take him on easy trails, hitch him up with an experienced dog that is not at all ski shy, or chase somebody else and make the experience exciting and fun.

Dogfights

Dogfights are not to be tolerated. Period. Do whatever you need to do to break up a fight and then severely discipline all parties. If your dog learns to behave around other dogs from puppyhood on, it helps immensely in preventing future fights. At about a year old, almost all dogs will go through a stage where they want to boss other dogs around. You need to convey that such behavior is not tolerable. Neutering can help a great deal, especially if done early.

If you have one dog that likes to fight, the other dogs seem to pick it up. If you acquire an adult dog that turns out to be a fighter, it might be best to return the dog and save yourself a lot of trouble. Sled dogs from established kennels often have already been taught that they are not allowed to fight. Good kennels raise high-quality dogs and a fight might injure or ruin an expensive dog, so fighting in the best kennels is not tolerated. Often, aggressive tendencies have been bred out.

Running puppies in a team is one exception to the no-aggression rule. Serious fights between pups should be broken up, but when you hook up an excited team of puppies or yearlings, often one pup will argue a little with the dog next to it. If it's not a serious altercation, you can let it slide. The habit usually disappears with training and age. You need to monitor the behavior of puppies, but you don't necessarily have to take their actions as seriously as you would those of an adult dog.

Aggressive Dogs

Some competitive dogs become aggressive going out of the starting chute—they will bite the dog next to them in their excitement. It's a tricky and sometimes very hard habit to break, because they are simply excited and you don't want to kill their enthusiasm. At the same time, you need to be concerned for the other dog's comfort and safety. Mari sees this play dominance more in the pointer crosses. Sometimes you can put an aggressive dog next to a dog that refuses to tolerate that behavior. As long as you are careful not to let retaliation escalate into a real fight, the retaliating dog may teach the aggressive one to behave. Other possibilities include shortening or lengthening the dog's tugline so that it's harder for him to pick on the other dog. Muzzling the dog is a possibility, but you must use a muzzle specifically designed for racing dogs (such as the ones greyhounds wear) so that your dog can breathe freely while running.

If you have an overly dominant dog, it's important that she acknowledge you as the boss. If you don't assert yourself, the dog will start running the show. Giving a dog a measure of freedom can be acceptable if the dog doesn't abuse the privilege; but no matter what, it's important to be consistent with commands and retain your position as the one who has final say over behavior and resources. Think of yourself as a "benevolent leader." You can be kind, positive, and gentle, but you are always in command.

Dogs that are aggressive toward other teams are a real problem on shared trails. If your dog or dogs act aggressively toward other dogs, work with a professional dog trainer if need be. Be sure to curb the problem before skijoring where you may meet other dogs. Sometimes just taking an obedience class will help with this problem.

Attitude Problems

A dog's desire to pull hard and to please you is a combination of training, ability, and attitude. Like ability, attitude often is an inborn trait, and some dogs just plain don't have it. Being a sled dog is not their idea of fun. (This dislike of pulling isn't limited to non-northern breeds, either. Some sled dogs don't want to be sled dogs.) Don't expect a dog to be a winner if he doesn't have the necessary drive, competitive spirit, and solid work ethic. Say, for example, you own a sweet, gentle-spirited dog that wants nothing more than to be by your side. It might be difficult to persuade him to leave your side and begin pulling like a champion.

You can't force attitude any more than you can force a dog to skijor. If you try to do so, the dog will become scared of you. If you really want to skijor, look for a dog that has the potential to pull. But keep in mind that although you can't create attitude where there is none, you can foster the seeds of good attitude by careful training and attention. You also can dampen a good attitude by excessive training, discipline that is too harsh, or insensitivity to the dog's needs.

If you find yourself running out of patience and losing your desire to work with a particular dog, a new home may be the best answer. Carol had a dog yard full of shy, insecure, soft-headed dogs that she received from exasperated dog drivers. She loved the challenge of gaining their trust and building up their confidence. Yet she gave away a perfectly adequate—but stubborn—dog because his bullheadedness drove her crazy. His new owner was delighted with him. What you consider a major liability may be someone else's favorite challenge.

Sour Dogs

If a dog appears to be sour on pulling—slacking off, taking wrong turns, misbehaving, or becoming generally unenthusiastic—look first for a medical problem. If a good puller suddenly doesn't want to run, it's not likely that it's a discipline problem. Sometimes a dog wants to perform but simply can't. Don't forget to look at the dog's feet. Check both the pads and the webbing between the pads. The foot may appear fine until you spread out the pad and discover deep fissures, or splits, in the webbing or the sides of the pads. Snowballs between the dog's pads will also affect a dog's running ability. If the feet seem fine, take the dog to the vet and have her checked for infections or injury. You may want to have a urine or blood sample analyzed. Low thyroid (hypothyroidism) is a known health issue in some sled-dog lines and an easy problem to fix.

If your dog checks out physically, it may be that he has been overtrained and needs a rest. He may be feeling too much pressure, or he has been asked to do new things that he is not yet ready for. Are you giving your dog adequate rest between runs? It's fine for a dog to come home a little tired, but he should still be perky and happy. Varying your training—different lengths and speeds, new trails, and easy runs interspersed with more serious training—is important for mental attitude. Perhaps you're training on the same trails all the time, and the dog is simply bored. Perhaps you are nagging too much: Can you imagine how you'd feel if somebody harped at you all the time? Your dog won't like it any more than you would. Perhaps you are not encouraging the dog enough, you're expecting too much, or you are going too fast for the dog. The dog may not have the potential to do what you want him to do.

DAVE PARTEE

A good roll after a run is always rejuvenating.

If a dog is too young to handle your level of expectations, she may burn out trying to meet them. If you race competitively with a nine-month-old pup, you may not have much of a dog left when she's two years old. It's better to let a dog mature before pushing her too hard.

If you wish to bring back a sour dog's attitude, you may have to lay off training for a week or do something totally different. Go skijoring on different trails or go out with a friend and have the dog chase somebody. Try to give the dog a good feeling about skijoring again. Dogs that become sour on home trails often perk up when they go somewhere else. If you run with a lead dog and two team dogs, the leader may need a break from the pressure of being up front.

Dogs That Won't Stop

Teach your dog to stop before you start skijoring with him. It's not difficult to teach a dog to halt or to lie down and stay—when you are not on skis. You have to be consistent and firm in teaching this. Use the summer months to reinforce your training.

Sometimes a previously trained dog gets excited the first time you go out on skis again after a summer off, and he completely forgets how to stop. Don't take this too seriously or overreact and damage the dog's enthusiasm. Give him slack the first couple of times. If he continues to misbehave, plan a few training sessions when your sole purpose is to remind him that he needs to stop and lie down even when you are skijoring.

Dogs That Don't Respond to Certain Commands

If you buy a dog that's already trained, be sure to ask what commands the dog knows. For example, some dogs are trained to pass another team or to go past a turnoff by the command "straight ahead," while others are taught "on by." (Some dogs are taught both.) You may find yourself calling "straight ahead!" at a dog that has no idea what the command means. It also makes sense to teach your own dogs common commands like "gee," "haw," and "whoa," so that if you lend or sell your dog, the new driver will be familiar with the same commands.

If you have trained the dog yourself, the problem may be that you haven't been clear or consistent in conveying what a certain command means. If the command requires a complex response, try to break it down into simpler parts and be sure the dog understands each level before you go on to the next.

For example, Carol taught her first skijoring dog the commands "gee over" and "haw over" because she was running Willow on a paved road at the time and wanted to be able to direct her off the road whenever cars appeared. She first taught the dog gee and haw, then taught her to move over to the side of a road or trail at the command "over," and finally put the two together to direct Willow to move over to a particular side. We find that the commands "gee over" and "haw over" are much easier taught on foot.

More Training Philosophy
Reading Your Dogs

If you watch them carefully, your dogs will tell you whole volumes about themselves, how they feel, what they think of your training (or what they think of you!), and what they need. Each dog is an individual, and you learn about each one through both training and experience. On your home trails, where most of your training takes place, you can learn how each dog is going to react to various situations and types of discipline. Sometimes, when you discover a training requirement your dogs don't like, you might have to be quite firm to get through that particular stage, but you and your dogs can also learn much in the process.

An unhappy or sour dog sometimes will communicate her displeasure by misbehaving or taking wrong turns. A leader that is burned out from the stress of leading also may begin deliberately

misbehaving. In both of these cases, it is better to address the root problem than to focus on the wrong turn. If a lively, enthusiastic dog suddenly becomes laid-back just before a run, this is a strong clue that the dog is not feeling well. Some dogs are the opposite— they don't seem particularly enthusiastic until you leave. Once you learn how the dog normally reacts, you can tune in to behavior that differs.

When you're running, your dog's ears can convey several things. If the ears are laid back a little, the dog is probably concentrating on the job at hand. If the ears are up, often the dog is not concentrating—or there's something going on up ahead. If your leaders suddenly perk up their ears, that often means there's something on the trail ahead that they can hear or smell long before you can. Often a dog's tail also comes up a little bit when something is distracting her. If the ears are working back and forth, the dog likely is unsure of something. Sometimes, after going by a squirrel or moose, a dog will start looking for more of them. When a dog's ears are up and forward a lot throughout a run, some drivers joke that the dog is "shopping."

For sprint dogs (dogs that run at a fast lope for relatively short distances of three to thirty miles), a general rule of thumb is that if a dog's tail or head is up, she's not working. If this happens suddenly, the most likely thing may be an injury. Or she may be next to a dog she doesn't like, or she may have had a negative experience on that part of the trail. Dogs have a long memory for where they have been, especially if something bad happened.

Dogs accustomed to long distances and slower speeds may hold their tails higher while they work, and in this case a lowered tail may signify fear or depression. But if a dog starts running with her head up, she may be either injured or nervous—or both. A change in gait may also signify injury.

Dogs communicate in many subtle ways. Their behavior, their facial expressions, their stance, even the manner in which they wag their tail—all can convey information on how they're feeling or what they're about to do next. Books on canine communication can greatly enhance your knowledge of your dog's behavior. But the best way to learn what your dog is saying is to watch her.

Never Stop Learning

Mari started mushing when she was fourteen years old and has had decades of experience as a competitive dog driver. Yet she still learns something every time she works with her dogs. If you keep your eyes open, you can learn something from a beginner as much as from someone who's been driving dogs for forty years. You might learn something from people who've never even been around dogs. If you are a competitive racer, you will discover that it's important to remain alert and open-minded even when you are winning. There's always someone out there who may be able to beat you. Pick up tidbits and file them away in your mind; use whatever works for you.

On the other hand, it's important to be firm and consistent. Being open to ideas doesn't mean you should change your habits every week based on some new piece of information. That confuses the dogs. Learning to drive dogs well is a process of taking in as much information as possible and processing it, evaluating it in terms of your own goals, priorities, and habits.

There's also a fine distinction between being open to new knowledge and being true to yourself. If you are a soft-handed person and someone you believe to be knowledgeable says you have to really push your dogs hard to get the most out of them, then you are faced with a decision. Can I change? Do I really believe in that philosophy? Every person is different, and your dog is accustomed to who you have been all along as his handler. That's the way he expects you to be. If you change too suddenly, your dog doesn't know what to expect and you've undermined his trust. If you abruptly switch to negative reinforcement when you've always focused on encouragement and praise, your dog may lie right down in the trail in response to the unaccustomed harshness. Conversely, a dog accustomed to a strong hand (which does not necessarily mean physical discipline but rather a forceful delivery of commands) may respond inappropriately to a too-soft approach.

This principle was graphically illustrated to Carol when she borrowed a friend's lead dog for a trial run. Yeti, a six-year-old male, had never been run by a woman before. He'd originally been trained as a long-distance dog and would naturally slow down to a trot if left to his own devices. Yeti's owner, Wes, advised Carol to say, "Yeti, hike!" in a strong, deep voice if the dog started to slow down.

Carol hitched up a small team to her sled, putting Yeti in double lead with her own rather soft-headed lead dog, Rissa. They did just fine until Carol said a word of encouragement in her normal dog-driving voice, which she pitches high and light. Yeti dropped to the ground like a stone, bringing the entire team to an abrupt halt. He'd come unglued at that utterly foreign sound. Carol managed to get the team going again, and as long as she kept her mouth shut, all went well. Then Yeti slowed down to a trot. Following Wes's advice, Carol called, "Yeti, hike!" in a deep, strong voice. This time Rissa hit the ground. Carol had never talked to her like that before. Nursing this duo back to the trailhead was a real challenge.

This is a bit of an extreme example, but it illustrates that we all have our own ways of driving dogs. It may take some time for a dog to adjust to a new driver's voice and ways.

Consistency and Discipline

Regardless of whether you are soft-handed or stern, your dogs should know that you are the leader at all times. It's all right to grant your dog a little freedom, but it's also important to be consistent when it counts. For example, when you are passing something on the trail, if you have given the dog a signal such as "straight ahead" and the dog tries to ignore you, don't give in. Make sure she goes by that distraction. Like kids, some dogs may occasionally test you to see if you mean what you say, and most dogs will test you more than once. Reinforcement is occasionally necessary.

Dogs draw security from clearly set guidelines. They are creatures of habit, descended from strongly social ancestors. They like consistency and are most comfortable when they have a strong and confident leader—you. Your dogs will trust you more if they always know what you expect from them—and what to expect from you.

Nonverbal communication can be a big part of dog training, but it can't take the place of spoken commands when your dogs are facing away from you and can't see what you're doing. True verbal communication works only when the participants agree on the meaning of the sounds they make. The word must mean the same thing every time: if "No!" means "Quit this very instant!" one time and "Oh, you probably shouldn't be doing that but I'm too lazy to make you stop" the next, you're breaking down the language. If the dog can't trust that when you say a certain word, you mean a certain word, then you won't have true communication because you don't always mean what you say.

Mari has learned a lot from training border collies, who often know ten different herding commands both by word and by whistle. You always use the same commands because if you change a command, the dog becomes confused and insecure. *Not enforcing a command is the same as changing it.* Along this line, discipline, if used consistently and humanely to reinforce language, builds the dog's trust and confidence.

Quality training counts more than quantity. You can work a dog four times a day, but if you aren't following through on your work, it will do no good. Once you have made the commitment to be your dog's teacher, you have taken on significant responsibility. Your dog looks to you as a leader, one who guides and directs the course of the dog's life. You will receive back what you invest in your student. If you are a consistent, dedicated, conscientious leader, you are likely to end up with an honest, hard-working

DAVE PARTEE

dog. If you lead carelessly and haphazardly, your dog likely will be inconsistent and unreliable. Ultimately, your dog is a mirror of yourself. It is up to you to choose what you want to reflect.

5 Putting It Together: Skijoring, Canicross, Bikejoring, and More

Once you and your dog have learned to skijor, the possibilities are endless. Whether you live in a snowy northern area or a region where snow is a luxury, you can work with your dog nearly year-round. The main limiting factor will be heat. No matter what activity you engage in, it's important to know your dog's tolerance

These dogs pull the laundry to the Laundromat every Thursday morning. A wagon kit converts the standard nursery wagon from people power to dog power.

DAPHNE LEWIS

for the combination of heat and exertion. Hard-working dogs can overheat at twenty degrees Fahrenheit above zero, let alone at sixty or seventy degrees. A dog that seems comfortable playing in the yard at sixty degrees Fahrenheit can become much hotter while pulling, because he is working at a higher level and with a more constant effort.

Training on different surfaces requires some adjustments to equipment and technique, but the basic principles remain the same. Start out gradually, with distances as short as a mile or two. If your dog is in great shape and shows no sign of fatigue after a run, you can increase the mileage fairly rapidly. But if your dog has not been working or playing regularly and is tired after a run, take things slowly. A good rule of thumb is to wait until a dog finishes happy and tail wagging, ready for more, before increasing your distance.

When you are finished with a run, be sure to offer your dog a drink of water and a snack or a dog treat along with lots of praise.

DAPHNE LEWIS

After a morning run in Georgia, these dogs drink water and cool off in a stream.

No matter how the run has gone (and it is inevitable that some will go badly), *always* end on a positive note. Finish with a good pat on the back for your partner. Letting your dog play and run around afterward is a good way to show your appreciation. It's also a good way to keep a dog from stiffening up if he has worked hard on the run. In the summer, many dogs love to cool off with a splash in a kiddie pool. If your route can incorporate a pit stop at a small stream, all the better.

Rest is just as important as exercise. As you and your dog build muscle and aerobic capacity, you both need breaks to allow your bodies to recover. A mix of activities and intensity levels is also beneficial both for building muscle and for avoiding boredom. If you go out for a hard run one day, spend the next day romping in the backyard, going for a long walk, or taking a swim together. For dogs who work year-round, taking a month or two off is a good idea, especially in the hottest months. If your dog works especially hard every winter, it's a good idea to treat him to a couple of months of easy, fun activities during the summer.

But for many skijorers, winter doesn't necessarily mean enough snow for skijoring. When snow is lacking, you may want to look

DAVE PARTEE

These dogs are pulling a Sacco cart, which includes a steering bar and a brake. When using shafts, it's important to choose dogs that have well-matched gaits.

into other forms of what is sometimes lumped together as "dryland skijoring" or, more broadly, "dryland mushing." These include canicross, bikejoring, scooters, and carts or gigs.

The simplest of these is canicross, which is running on foot with your dog pulling you. The equipment is virtually the same: a regular pulling harness for the dog, a skijoring line, and a skijoring belt. Running coaches (not to mention physical therapists and your own body) will tell you it's best to be able to swing both arms freely, so holding a leash in one hand is not recommended. Using a belt and a skijoring line with a good bungee in it is far preferable to wearing out first one arm and then the other as you try to hold a leash and run. However, you may find that a shorter skijoring line works better when you're on foot. Carol uses a short skijoring line that puts her dog about five or six feet ahead of her. In canicross, the benefits of a comfortable, low-riding belt will become even more evident than in skijoring.

If you are already a runner, and your dog has been a certified couch potato, it is entirely possible to outpace or outdistance your dog. Watch carefully for signs of fatigue, and pay close attention to your dog's gait. Don't assume your dog is ready to leap right

DAVE PARTEE

into a five-mile run just because you are. On the other hand, you may have just gotten yourself off the coach while your dog has been running laps in the backyard, and this is where "easy" may become your favorite command until your dog learns to pace himself to your speed. Most dogs can learn to differentiate between the pace of canicross and the pace of skijoring, though some seem more suited to it than others. A friend of ours does canicross with her big, powerful lead dog every summer. Buddy—who weighs about sixty pounds and could easily pull Andrea off her feet—quickly learned that summer and canicross mean a much more sedate pace than winter and twenty-mile-per-hour sprints. On the other hand, a hyperactive dog that is way too focused on pulling hard would not be a good choice for canicross.

If you don't have easy access to dirt roads or trails, you may have no choice but to run on sidewalks or paved roads. Running on asphalt should be done cautiously and conscientiously. If it's too hot for you to walk barefoot on the asphalt, it's too hot for your dog to run on it. Carefully monitor your dog's feet to make sure his pads are tolerating the abrasive surface. Some people use Cordura or other protective cloth booties to preserve their dog's feet. Asphalt can also radiate heat, so keep a close eye on your dog to make sure he's not overheating.

Bikejoring, while quite popular in some areas, is more complicated than canicross and also can be more hazardous. Good equipment, protective gear, and a large dose of common sense are required, as are well-trained dogs. We've heard many stories of spectacular crashes caused by squirrels, loose dogs, cats, and other irresistible distractions. You will need to adjust your speed to conditions and maintain control at all times. A well-trained dog that responds quickly to your voice is essential, and the commands "easy" and "stay" may become lifesavers. You should be proficient at biking and have good balance before you add a hard-pulling dog.

There are many opinions about the best way to attach your dog to your bike, and several different pieces of equipment that can be used. The primary consideration should always be safety. Does the attachment prevent the line from being tangled in the wheels or in the pedals? Is there a spring in the attachment that will help absorb the shock of a strong pull? Does the point of attachment leave you in full control of your bike, or does it pull you to one side or the other? Can you steer without any problem regardless of which way a dog may bolt? Does the line interfere in any way with your ability to brake?

Attaching a line to the front end of your bike by looping it below the handlebar stem will allow the dog a great deal of pulling power, so should only be done if you are an accomplished bike rider. A side-mount attachment is safer for exercising dogs and is designed to keep the dog from using his full pulling strength. If your goal is exercise and sanity, and you don't plan to race or train hard, go for the kind that keeps the dog from pulling too much.

The book *Ski Spot Run* by Matt Haakenstad and John Thompson has an excellent description of bikejoring and is recommended

DAVE PARTEE

reading if you decide you would like to try this exciting but challenging activity. The authors recommend that before you try bikejoring with a dog, ask a friend to pull you around on your bike so you can practice braking to slow your speed, climbing and descending small hills, turning quickly, and stopping.

Other popular dryland activities include being pulled on a scooter, cart, or wheeled rig. Dog scootering is similar to bikejoring, but the driver uses a kick scooter with a brake and can help the dog by pedaling with one foot. The dog is attached to the front of the scooter with a tugline or gangline. As with bikejoring and canicross, be mindful of the surface your dog is running on. Choose dirt roads or trails whenever possible, and if you must run your dog on asphalt, be vigilant about monitoring your dog's feet and the air temperature.

Dog rigs, also known as gigs or carts, can accommodate anywhere from one to multiple dogs. They may have two, three, or

HOWLING DOG ALASKA

Dogs take a break during their first scooter run of the season. Running short distances and taking frequent breaks are a must during early-season or warm-weather training.

four wheels. Some are designed for sitting while others require the driver to stand, and some allow the driver to pedal. Some two-wheeled dogcarts are designed to use shafts that are very similar to the shafts used in Nordic-style dog mushing (see chapter 9). Dog mushers in the United States often use rigs to train dog teams during the summer, and gig racing is a common sport in many countries all over the world. The Web is a great place to learn more about dryland mushing.

As we've said before, the paramount consideration for any kind of dog-powered sport should always be safety. For that reason, one activity we hesitate to recommend is rollerjoring, which involves the use of inline skates or rollerskis. Rollerjoring is probably the most dangerous form of dryland skijoring. If you are not proficient on inline skates, or your dog is untrained, the potential for injury skyrockets. Please do not attempt this activity unless your dog knows and responds reliably to commands, you've done cani-cross, you're thoroughly proficiency at inline skating, and you've extensively practiced quick braking and sudden maneuvers *without* the dog. You should always wear a helmet and full protective

This three-wheeled gig has a gap between the two footboards, so the driver can pedal to help the dogs if needed.

DAPHNE LEWIS

This simple sulky is lightweight and easy for dogs to pull. The seat is positioned well behind the wheel axles so that when the driver sits in the seat, the shaft tip lifts up on the harness. The larger dog is pulling from the front of the shaft, and the smaller dog is pulling with a tugline that goes to the back of the shaft.

gear, and you should practice with a leash or tow bar (so that you can let go in an emergency) in a safe, zero-traffic area until you are completely confident you can handle any situation that may arise.

For all dryland activities, remember that the basic principles and training techniques are similar. Wear protective gear if appropriate. Make sure your wheeled rig—in whatever form it takes—has good working brakes. If you are doing canicross, make sure you can safely control your dog power on foot—which includes avoiding downhill runs until you are confident of your ability to regulate your dog's speed. Start out conservatively until you are familiar with the techniques and the potential pitfalls of the type of dog driving you are attempting. Always monitor your dog's attitude and physical condition, as well as your own. And remember that dog driving in any of its numerous forms should be fun for both you and your dog. If, after giving a particular activity a good try, you find that one of you simply isn't enjoying the experience, switch activities until you find one that suits you both.

6

Trails and Trail Etiquette

Skijorers lucky enough to have their own trails enjoy the luxury of privacy. How they train on and maintain their home trails is a personal decision. But sooner or later, most skijorers will find themselves on a trail used by others. When you skijor on public or shared trails, two considerations come into play: public image and compatible use.

Public Image

Most sports have a certain image with the general public. Hockey, for instance, is often seen as a fast-moving but violent sport. The public's image of, say, baseball or gymnastics is far different from its image of hockey or football.

The general public's image of dog driving is complicated by the presence of the dog. Cross-country skiing as a sport is not particularly controversial, unless you count the controversy between the merits of skating versus diagonal striding in competition. But dog driving, whether with a sled or on skis, is haunted by a debate over whether it is cruel to make a dog pull a sled or skier. Those of us who drive dogs know full well that we don't force our dogs to pull. In fact, for a husky born and bred to pull, the greatest punishment a dog driver can dole out is to leave that dog behind.

But there are those who, from lack of adequate information, think we are mistreating our dogs by "forcing" them to pull us. (We wonder whether these people have ever walked an enthusiastic dog on a leash.) Others feel that the pulling part is acceptable, but that dog drivers are too hard on the dogs. Every time a dog musher or skijorer abuses a dog, and every time a dog dies while in harness, the whole sport of dog driving suffers.

Because of this, it is vital that we who skijor take steps to prevent such occurrences and to foster a positive image of our sport. Here are a few general principles to keep in mind:

- Use common sense and restraint when you have to correct your dog's behavior in front of an audience. Abusive treatment is *never* justified, and privacy does not give you the right to mistreat your dog. However, an uninformed onlooker can misconstrue even humane and fair discipline.

- Learn constructive forms of correcting behavior and use positive reinforcement rather than negative whenever possible. Kicking or hitting your dog not only harms the image of skijoring but is counterproductive as well. You are likely to do far more harm than good in terms of training, plus you run the risk of injuring or frightening your dog. There are other more effective methods of discipline. Positive techniques for correcting your dog's behavior can be found in many dog-training books.

- Don't scream at a dog, whether it is your own or someone else's. Irate, screaming skijorers don't convey positive impressions to the general public. Yelling is also unnecessary. Your tone of voice conveys more to the dog than its volume.

- If confronted by a concerned individual who questions why you are making your dog pull you on skis, try some gentle persuasion. Invite that person to watch you skijor or even to try it out. It's difficult to maintain the argument that a dog is being forced to pull when that same dog is so obviously eager to get going. Also, listen carefully to the arguments presented. Often, sympathetic listening can disarm your critic. Try not to engage in a lengthy debate while you're out training your dog, however, because it's not good for the dog.

Compatible Use

When you venture onto a trail that is not your own, compatible use becomes an important issue. A public trail may be shared by dog mushers, horseback riders, snowmachiners, bicyclists, hikers, and skiers. Even if the trail is a dedicated-use trail and all the users are skijorers, any shared use requires courtesy and consideration.

Multiuse trails have both pros and cons. The pros are that trail maintenance can be shared, more voices can speak up for and protect access to that trail, and you may have a better chance of finding help if you run into trouble. The biggest drawback is that users may have incompatible needs for that trail. A horseback rider, for instance, can destroy a dog-mushing trail if the hard-packed snow isn't strong enough to keep the horse's hooves from punching through. On Carol's home trails, bicyclists sometimes ride down the trail when the snow is too soft to handle the weight. The deep, twisting gullies left by their tires are hard on the dogs and a nightmare to navigate on skis.

Snowmachiners make great trail groomers if they drive slowly and carefully, but those who drive recklessly or at dangerously high speeds often gouge the trail—and they may not be able to avoid colliding with a dog team. Such accidents have resulted in dog injuries and even deaths. Snowmachiners who think it's fun to crisscross or jump over a groomed dog trail cause a real mess, and snowmachines that take bumps at high speeds create horrible moguls.

Conversely, skijorers can pose a hazard to other users. Dog mushers have gotten hopelessly entangled with skijoring teams that lost control of their dogs or failed to pull far enough off the trail. Hikers and skiers are at risk if an out-of-control skijorer collides with them. Dogs tend to frighten horses when they meet unexpectedly. And unfriendly or unruly skijoring dogs can cause major problems for all other users.

Sharing a trail with others can work successfully only if done with courtesy and consideration. Good trail etiquette is vital if you wish to be welcomed by fellow trail users.

Trail Etiquette Tips

Always maintain full control of your dogs, both on and off the trail. *In any situation that may arise, you are fully and absolutely responsible for your dog's behavior.* If your dog is a fighter, it is your responsibility to keep him away from other dogs, no matter what it takes to do so. If your dogs are unruly when passing or being passed, either train them to behave, move your dogs completely off the trail when a team passes you, or stay off public trails altogether. "I just couldn't control my dogs" is never an acceptable excuse for causing problems to other trail users.

A corollary to this is that you shouldn't skijor with more dogs than you can handle. Besides creating a menace on the trail, it teaches the dogs bad habits and undermines your authority. Even open-class dog mushers, who will eventually race with twelve or more dogs in their team, start out each new training season with small, easily controlled teams. By the time a musher works up to a large team, actual physical control becomes an illusion, but an illusion that must be rock-solid in the dogs' heads. Control is essential no matter what the size of the team.

Do not allow your dogs to run loose around other skijorers or mushers, whether on the trail, trailhead, or holding area. Even if your dog is well behaved, the mere fact that he's loose will excite the other dogs and make it more difficult for their handlers to control them. If you need proof of this, ask any musher what happens in his kennel when a dog gets loose or a strange dog comes into the yard. It drives the other dogs crazy (which is an effective way to find the weak links in your tie-out chains or fence).

Don't take your dog on a leash to watch the start of a race or observe other teams heading down the trail. At a race, your dog will be a most unwelcome distraction to the competing dogs and drivers. Even during training, your dog's presence may cause problems for other skijorers or mushers. In general, it's best to discourage visiting between dog teams. Unless invited, don't take your dog to say hello to the team next door. Whenever other people are present at a trail you are using, don't turn your dogs loose. Even a friendly dog may frighten someone who has had a bad experience.

If you train at a public trail with a large holding area and multiple teams using the trail at one time, watch what the other teams are doing. Don't start out at the same time as another team or skijorer. If an eight-dog team is being hooked up and is almost ready to roll, by all means wait a few minutes and let it go out first. Also, try not to interfere with incoming teams. Wait for them to clear the trailhead before going out.

If you train at night, make sure you can be seen. Put reflective tape on your dog's harness and your own clothing, and wear a headlamp.

Last, we know of dog drivers who like to listen to tunes while they're running dogs. For your own safety and the safety of those around you, you need to be able to hear clearly. Leave the headphones behind.

Once you are out on the trail, the basic principle of right-of-way is this: The person with the fewest dogs usually has the most control and therefore should yield right of way to the other. To boil this down to the smallest teams, if a one-dog skijorer meets a two-dog skijorer, the one-dogger should yield.

You are responsible for untangling your own dogs. If a six-dog mushing team gets tangled with your two-dog skijoring team, don't expect the other driver to sort your dogs out.

When tangles or other mishaps occur, it's easy to get upset. Keep your temper and always be courteous, *even if the other driver is not.* Work as quietly and calmly as possible. It doesn't matter whether you're wrong or right; the welfare of the dogs comes first, and you shouldn't upset them. If you and the other driver need to discuss the mishap, do it later.

If another driver needs help during a mishap or tangle and accepts your offer of assistance, by all means lend a hand. However, don't intrude if the driver refuses your assistance, and be extremely careful when handling other people's dogs. A tangled dog may panic, and any panicked dog is potentially dangerous. Talk to the dog in low, friendly, soothing tones. Avoid quick, jerky movements. If a dog is unmanageable or acts at all aggressively toward you, let his driver work with him.

Never turn a tangled dog loose, not even your own pet. A dog under stress from a tangle may run away or cause added trouble. Our local dog-mushing e-mail list in Fairbanks has seen innumerable posts over the years about lost dogs who were normally reliable but got loose during a tangle and took off in fright.

When you are skijoring, ski on the same side of the trail as your dog is running so that you don't pose a hazard to others. If you stop on the trail, move both yourself and your dog well over to one side so that others can pass you safely and easily.

If you are passed, hold your dogs back and allow the team ahead to get back up to speed. Wait for a few minutes to put distance between you and the passing team. Many dogs become nervous when followed too closely.

When you come up behind someone and wish to pass, holler "trail!" well ahead of time to warn of your presence. Be courteous and careful. There is no set rule for passing on the right or left, so watch the team ahead and pass on whichever side is available.

If the team you are passing is spread out all over the trail and you become tangled while trying to get by, or if the other team refuses to yield the trail, this is not an appropriate time to educate the other driver in trail etiquette. Discuss it later, and please be gentle. Many beginners unknowingly breach etiquette and are crushed when they are promptly and unmercifully chewed out by an irate driver.

Train your dog to ignore all distractions, including loose dogs, moose, skiers, snowmachines, or other teams on the trail. Charlie Champaine, an Alaska sprint-mushing champion, said he welcomed distractions on his training runs. He treated each incident as an opportunity to teach his dogs to ignore everything but the job at hand. It's a good attitude to cultivate, and the training will pay off in having a team that is a delight to run.

Don't allow your male dog to stop and mark the trail indiscriminately. His signature on a tree or snowbank will tempt other males to stop and add their own mark. A pit stop is reasonable on a longer outing. Stopping every thirty feet to mark a new tree is not. If you are on ski trails or in a high-traffic area of a public trail, clean up after your dog.

Don't bring sick dogs to a public trail. If you know your dogs have an infectious disease, please keep them home until they're no longer contagious. Passing on and contracting diseases at public trails is unavoidable, and it can serve to boost your dogs' immunities, but don't pass on a disease deliberately.

Always clean up your holding area or dog-drop site. Dog feces are not just unpleasant to look at; they can harbor worms and viruses that will infect any dog that sniffs at a contaminated pile. Bring a shovel and a bag every time you run at a public trail or travel with your dogs. Clean up all people trash as well. This includes cigarette butts and food items. Leave your spot as clean as or cleaner than you found it.

Where to Find Trails

In some areas, finding a good dog trail is simply a matter of asking a fellow skijorer or contacting your nearest dog-mushing or skijoring club. (Numerous North American dog-driving clubs are listed with the International Sled Dog Racing Association; see the Resources at the back of this book.) Other potential resources for trail information include snowmachine clubs, ski clubs, your area's parks and recreation department, and (in the United States) the federal Bureau of Land Management.

Don't assume you are welcome on all dog-mushing trails just because you drive dogs. Always check with whoever maintains the trail before you venture onto a dedicated dog-mushing race track. Some mushing clubs have given skijorers a warm welcome and have found the ensuing relationship to hold many rewards and few problems. But not all dog-driving clubs allow skijorers on their trails. Keep in mind that if you do use a dedicated dog-mushing trail, practicing good etiquette is absolutely essential if you want to be invited back.

If you live in an urban area, finding a place to skijor can be a bit tricky. Be careful not to start out on the nearest groomed ski trail! Dogs are banned from most dedicated ski trails. Ask first, and make sure your canine friend is welcome. In Anchorage and Fairbanks, skijorers worked out an arrangement with ski clubs and ski-trail groomers so they could skijor on a dedicated ski trail at designated times. This compromise is a vast improvement over ignoring a dog ban and making yourself permanently unwelcome.

Golf courses and city parks, beaches, lakes, or ponds all are potential areas for skijoring. Using private golf courses usually will require permission, but they may be an ideal solution if you receive the go-ahead. National and state parks can be wonderful places to skijor; again, check first if at all possible to find good trails and establish your welcome. Some ski resorts have added skijoring trails, but be sure you find out which trails are acceptable to use.

Use extreme caution when skijoring on waterways. Test the ice first to make sure it will hold your weight. Make sure you can quickly release your skijoring line so that if your dog or you fall through the ice, you won't both get dragged in. Don't skijor alone on ice if you can help it, and always let someone know where you are going and when you expect to return.

ANDREA SWINGLEY

Skijorers received special permission to use the Birch Hill ski trails in Fairbanks, Alaska, for world championship skijoring and Nordic-style races in 2001.

Back roads are always a possibility for skijorers, as are dead-end streets, ballparks, and bike paths. In most cases, you'll have to keep an eye out for loose dogs, a common drawback to skijoring in populated areas. You may also have to watch for poor snow conditions or trails that have been plowed down to the pavement. With a little advance planning, however, skijoring in an urban area can be as much fun as skijoring out in the wild.

Making Your Own Trails

If you have access to a snowmachine, you may want to blaze your own skijoring trails. Or you may find it possible to co-op on a new trail with other potential trail users, such as snowmachiners or dog mushers. In the Fairbanks area, skijorers, dog mushers, the U.S. Army Corps of Engineers, and the local parks and recreation department worked together to create a series of winter trails in a floodplain.

There are numerous methods for creating and maintaining such trails. Many dog-mushing trails are groomed by snowmachine, with a heavy drag towed behind the snowmachine that packs and smoothes out the trail base. Some trails are maintained with specialized track vehicles. Ask a few experienced trail groomers for advice if you want something other than a narrow snowmachine trail.

If you make your own trail, please be sure you don't run it across someone's private property without permission. All too

In Fairbanks, members of the local skijoring club groom trails with a snowmachine and drag.

often, trail makers simply follow the path of least resistance, violating the rights of property owners in the process. If you can receive permission to run your trail on state or federal land, you may be able to avoid such problems as trespassing, road crossings, and inconvenient plowing schedules.

Cooperating with other trail users has an additional benefit besides the potential manpower. The added voices, working together, can speak up to protect a new or existing trail from encroachment by roads and buildings. A state legislature or local transportation department may prove far more willing to accommodate a host of trail users than to make modifications for a single group. A great example is the Goldstream Public Use Area in Fairbanks. Its designation as a protected area was scheduled to expire, but so many different user groups spoke up in its favor that it was granted permanent protected status.

If you belong to a skijoring or dog-mushing club that maintains trails, please donate to the grooming effort. Setting and maintaining a good trail can take hours of work and a fair amount of fuel. Consider donating some of your time, too. Grooming trail can be lots of fun, especially with company, and the rewards are tangible.

DAVE PARTEE

7 Dog Care and Feeding

The kind of care you give a dog dictates his health, performance, happiness, and safety. If you take mediocre care of your dog, expect mediocre results. Ensuring your dog is comfortable, well fed, and healthy is an investment well worth making if you want the best from and for that dog.

Shelter

If your dog lives outside, it's important that his doghouse is well built and windproof, with no holes or gaps. If the dog has a thick coat, you provide warm bedding in the winter, and your winter temperatures are relatively moderate, the house doesn't necessarily have to be insulated. In Fairbanks, where temperatures drop to minus forty degrees Fahrenheit or below, even thick-coated dogs appreciate an insulated house. The house should have enough room for the dog to turn around and lie down inside but should be small enough to heat with his body. Mari's doghouses are about thirty-two by twenty-four inches and fully insulated on the inside, with a swinging Lexan (hard, clear plastic) door and a removable roof. There is enough clearance between the door opening and the door so that a chain won't get stuck. She has found that all her dogs, including the dogs in her boarding kennel, learn to use the swinging door with a little time and food treats. The removable roof (which rests on two-by-two-inch braces, without being permanently nailed) makes it easy to clean bedding out of the house in the springtime. The doorway is framed with two-by-four-inch boards to create a wind and snow break and to keep the dog from chewing out the doorway. The house is raised up from the ground on two-by-two-inch supports to keep it out of the mud and snow.

Carol's doghouses have insulation added to the exterior all the way around (top, bottom, and all sides), so the interiors of her houses are a little larger than Mari's. Like Mari's, most of her houses have a swinging Lexan door. For two of her dogs who flatly refused to use the hard plastic doors, she substituted a piece of thick, winter-weight rubber that stays flexible even in extreme cold. Carol

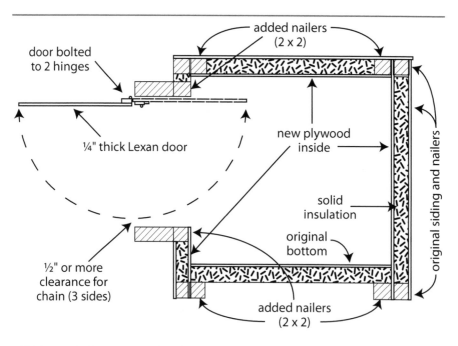

This is a vertical cross section for adding insulation and a swinging door to a 24-by-24-by-32-inch doghouse.

GREG SELLENTIN

Blue foam added to all sides, the floor, and the roof can raise the temperature inside a dog's house by as much as 29 degrees F above the outside ambient temperature when it's very cold. Adding a door raises the temperature even more and also provides extra protection from wind and precipitation.

likes to put overhanging roofs on her doghouses, because they help shelter the doorway from rain and snow. We both use flat-roofed doghouses so that the dogs can sun themselves on their roofs in the spring and can get up out of the mud in wet weather.

Whatever style of doghouse you choose, the door should not be too big. Most dogs like to go into a small cave and enjoy being able to hide in their doghouse. The door opening should be located up from the bottom floor, perhaps halfway up the front wall, so snow doesn't come in the doorway and bedding doesn't fall out. Carol prefers to locate the door to one side of the front wall, rather than in the center, so the dog can get out of the wind once inside.

Most huskies will chew anything within reach, including their doghouses. It's an ongoing battle—and the owner seems to be on the losing end more often than not—but you can try spray-on antichewing compounds, or perhaps find a special nontoxic paint that will discourage chewing. Putting a metal edge around the door opening works well. Another remedy that has worked well for some dog owners is pepper water, which can be made by mixing together dried chilies and water in a blender. Commercial hot sauce does not seem to be nearly as effective, and in fact, many years ago Carol lived with a puppy who thought hot sauce was a great condiment.

Generally, short-haired dogs should live inside or in a heated space such as a garage or dog barn during the winter to prevent early arthritis and early aging. Short-haired dogs aren't really suited to cold climates and require extra pampering. Dogs that can't live in the house will need an insulated doghouse with a door of some kind. Some people use heat lamps, but we don't recommend this because it's difficult to set them up so that they can't be broken or ignite a fire. Others have successfully used a special outdoor-grade heating pad that lies on the doghouse floor or a well-protected heater that hangs on the side wall of the doghouse.

If a dog won't use a hard plastic door, hanging a blanket or a piece of rug in front of the doghouse door also helps hold in the heat, as long as the dog doesn't eat it. Most huskies will eat whatever is in front of them, but we know of several people who successfully hang a blanket in the doghouse door for their Labrador retrievers.

Bedding

Regardless of whether or not you use insulated houses, your dogs should be bedded with an insulating material for the cold winter months. However, it's a common mistake to put in bedding too early in the fall, while it's still raining instead of snowing. The bedding gets moist as the dog goes in and out of the house when it rains. When it begins to freeze, that moisture turns to ice. Soon the dog starts lying outside because he doesn't want to sleep on the ice. It can be better for the dog—if he has a good undercoat and thick outer coat—to wait to add bedding until the snow comes. If your dog seems to be getting cold but it's still damp out, add bedding but change it out regularly, and start with all fresh bedding once the snow falls. Wood shavings sometimes make a good interim bedding until the weather turns really cold.

Most dog drivers use straw for winter bedding, but some dogs are allergic to it and need to be bedded with hay instead. You can also use both, putting down straw as the bottom layer and adding hay on the top. Moisture then passes through the hay, and the straw makes a good underlying cushion. Use high-quality bedding, with no foxtails or barley hulls. Oat or wheat straw works well. Be sure the bale is not damp, dusty, or moldy. If you store bedding for future use, be sure to keep it dry.

The ideal way to bed down a dog would be to clean out the old bedding every time you put in the new, and with one or two dogs, it's easy to do so. But those who keep several dogs often don't have the time, and we've found it works quite well to add fresh straw on top of the old during the cold winter months. Start with a sufficient layer of bedding. We both begin with a foundation of at least two flakes (two sections from a bale) of straw or hay in each doghouse to create a good cushion. Shake out the flakes so that the bedding fluffs up for better insulation. For subsequent layers, you can add a new flake on top of the old bedding about once every week or so, depending on the temperatures and how much straw your dog kicks out of the house.

Some people purchase a single bale of straw for the entire winter and put in fresh bedding perhaps twice all season. That's not adequate. If you want your dog to perform well, he must be able to conserve his energy for running and pulling, not for staying warm. He will also require less food if his house is warm and dry.

Most dogs don't require bedding during the summer. In the spring, you should take out all the old straw or hay. Not only is it dirty and itchy for the dog, but it is a wonderful medium for growing lice and mold. Sometimes the straw will even sprout or begin to decompose. Some dogs refuse to sleep in their doghouse once the winter bedding is removed. Carol has found that a thick layer of shavings usually will entice them. She mixes a very small amount of cedar shavings with a generous helping of spruce shavings. The cedar shavings help to keep down bugs, have a clean smell, and seem to resist mold and moisture problems fairly well. In Alaska's semiarid Interior, shavings often stay clean and dry all summer, so Carol puts straw in right on top of them for the winter and then cleans out everything in the spring. But if you live in a damp climate and the shavings have gotten damp or dirty, clean them out before putting in winter bedding.

Dog-Yard Maintenance

Securing the Dog

We do not advocate letting dogs run loose, and in many places it is mandatory to keep your dogs restrained. Some people prefer to keep their dogs in pens or a fenced yard, some use cable dog runs, and some prefer tie-out chains. If the dog is chained, the chain should be long enough to allow the dog to move around freely, but not so long that the dog can become tangled in objects around the yard. Be sure your dog can't strangle himself on a nearby fence. (Rope is not a suitable restraint, because it can be chewed apart in minutes.)

The chain can be attached to a post or tie-out stake. Some people use a pipe-and-rebar swivel system to keep the chain off the ground and to prevent tangles. Others have used sunken car axles to anchor their dog chains. The ultra-low-budget method, of course, is to use a tree. If you use a tree, keep in mind that the tree isn't likely to survive the chafing.

If your chain is around a post or tree, be careful to dig out the chain when it snows and to break it loose if it ices up, or it will get shorter and shorter until your dog is on a one-foot choke chain. Elevating the chain helps to prevent the dog from getting tangled

The white plastic piece between the rebar and the post in this swivel system helps reduce the noise of metal on metal. Flat-roofed houses make great lookout posts for curious dogs.

and keeps the chain free of snow. Longer chains should have a swivel in the middle of the chain.

Keep in mind that a longer chain will not give the dog more exercise, nor will a pen give her more exercise than a chain unless she has a playmate in the pen. A study done by Lloyd A. Delude and published in the July 1991 issue of *Team & Trail* showed that the dogs studied spent more than 80 percent of their time lying down, regardless of whether they were in a pen, on a cable run, or on a chain. When they did move, he found, they chose to walk more than 90 percent of the time. In other words, if you want your dogs to get more exercise, you will have to provide them with motivation, not longer chains. If you have multiple dogs, tie them far enough apart so they can't get tangled in each other's chains. If you have two dogs who don't get along, be careful that they can't even reach each other's feet, or you may find a dog missing some toes! The safest way to space them is so they can't touch at all.

Dogs enjoy having their own sacred spot to live in, and it's important that they feel confident and secure.

When you use chain or cable, make sure you use high-quality snaps and keep extra chain and snaps on hand. Be sure your snaps have swivels. Otherwise, the chain can twist up on the dog. Keep an eye on the condition of your hardware. Check occasionally to make sure chain and snap swivels are working smoothly. Snaps may need to be changed as often as once a year, depending on the dog. It always seems that if one dog's snap breaks, the other dogs' snaps will break at the same time. This often happens in the spring, when the dogs have become antsy at being laid off and are still in peak physical condition.

Regularly check each dog's collar to make sure it is neither too tight nor too loose. If you have an escape artist, be sure his collar is too snug to back out of. For true pinheads, putting on two collars,

In this dog yard just north of Fairbanks, bedding added to doghouses throughout the long winter creates large circles in each dog's area. In the spring, the dogs love to sun themselves on the warm straw.

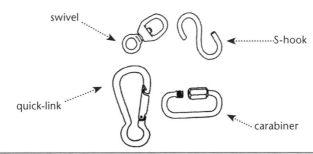

typical dog yard hardware

with the snap attached to the inner collar, sometimes does the trick. If one of your dogs figures out how to release snaps, use a covert snap or a quick link and swivel instead.

If you keep dogs loose in a pen or in the house, it is still important to give each dog its own little area or house. When you put more than one dog in a pen with only one house, the dominant dog may kick the other dog out in the cold.

Layout

Position your dog's house and tie-out area in a dry, well-drained spot that won't fill with water in the spring. Make sure you dig out the doorway of the doghouse when the snow gets deep. Dig far enough below the doorway so that the dog's chain doesn't drag chunks of snow into the house. As an alternative, dig the house out completely and set it on top of the snow. If possible, remove snow from the dog yard each spring, before it melts into dog-yard lakes.

Dogs should have a well-shaded area in the summer. Free access to fresh water is important in the warmer months. In the winter, as long as you water the dogs once or twice a day, they can get by without a constant supply of fresh water. But in the summer, their water dish should always be full.

For a secure water dish, some people nail a coffee can to the side of the doghouse. The can should be filled with fresh water every day, and you should be sure to empty the can completely at least several times a week (daily is ideal). Regularly wash out any dirt or algae. Mari adds a drop of Clorox to a big barrel of water in the summer, which also keeps out algae. If you want to be fancy, you can build a metal frame onto the side of the doghouse and place a bowl inside the frame. (A wooden frame may work but won't be chewproof.) Some dog-product catalogs carry prefabricated steel bowls and frames that can be mounted on a doghouse.

What's under your dog's feet is as important a consideration as what is over her head. Living ground cover quickly disintegrates under a dog's feet. Lawn or pasture turns to dirt, which then turns to mud in the rain. Gravel or road fill is an alternative, but some dogs eat rocks—and habitual rock eaters have an uncanny ability to dig down and find them even if you take out all the rocks on the surface. Larger rocks can lodge in the dog's stomach or intestine, which can prove fatal. If you own a confirmed rock eater, you may want to build a wooden platform for the dog. It can be initially expensive, but it may save you from a several-hundred-dollar vet bill or even a dead dog.

If you can afford it, using finer gravel may work—smaller rocks apparently pass through the dog's system more safely—but even small rocks can puncture a stomach wall. Carol uses a combination of sand and wood chips in her dog yard and replenishes the wood chips about once every other year, depending on the dog. Giving the dogs something else to chew on, like beef or rawhide bones, can help distract rock eaters and diggers. If you give bones, however, be aware that they come with their own potential drawbacks. They can get stuck in the dog's teeth, throat, or intestines. Don't use pig, lamb, or poultry bones because they are more brittle and tend to splinter. To avoid jealousy in your yard, make sure each dog has the same size bone. Some dogs like to excavate their areas in the summer, and there are varying philosophies about whether this should be discouraged or not. Some people go to great lengths to prevent holes in the yard, but some feel that hole digging is a natural distraction during the long summer months.

Cleanup

Cleaning up the dog yard is—or should be, anyway—a daily chore. If you develop the habit of cleaning up your dogs' feces every morning or every night (twice a day is even better), the chore is a minor one that takes only a few minutes. The best time to clean seems to be right after the dogs have been given their morning water, when they are calmest, or after the evening meal. If you use cleanup as a time to visit with each dog, it can become a positive task rather than drudgery.

Cleaning the yard only becomes a major headache if you leave it too long. A dirty dog yard is a great breeding ground for worms and diseases, and it does not make a particularly pleasant environment for either you or the dogs. A clean yard also cuts down on stool eating. If you can do so, move the dogs to a clean area once in a while and sterilize the old yard. Ask your veterinarian for advice on sterilization methods.

An old bucket and a shovel work well for dog-yard cleanup. A rectangular bucket turned on its side and cut on the diagonal, with a handle attached to the bottom, and paired with a small garden hoe, makes a great cleanup tool. Dog waste can be composted and used in gardens, although it is not recommended for using in vegetable gardens. Several kinds of dog-waste composting products and systems are available, and the U.S. Department of Agriculture has produced a handbook on composting dog waste (see the Bibliography at the back of this book, or go online and search on "composting dog waste"). If you don't have the means for composting and can't dispose of your dog manure on your own property (preferably in a deep hole and downwind of any neighbors), you can line a bucket with a trash bag for convenient trash pickup and/or transporting to the town dump. Many dog drivers save their old dog-food bags for cleanup around the yard and at trailheads.

Feeding and Watering
Feed

A skijoring dog should be fed well all year long. Whether you are going on trips or racing competitively, the dog is a working dog and needs top-quality dog food. This investment will pay off in the long run. Some people provide meat, either by itself or mixed with commercial dog food, while others prefer to feed one of the high-quality commercial dog foods that are nutritionally complete.

In the winter, and particularly in colder climates, the dog needs about 30 percent protein and at least 20 percent fat (by dry weight) in its diet. If your dog food doesn't have that percentage of fat in it, and you live in a cold area, add fat to the diet. If your dogs are too thin, you also may want to add fat—in moderation—to their diet. Some feed stores carry fats specifically designed for supplementing dog food.

If you plan to feed meat, chicken, beef, or horsemeat works well. Some drivers use meat products commercially produced for dogs or foxes. Liver is an excellent supplement, but only in small amounts (less than four ounces a day). If you want to add additional protein to your dog's ration, either fresh or powdered eggs are a good source. You also can add wheat germ oil, vitamins, and other supplements to increase the nutritional value of the diet.

If you have just two or three dogs, mixing your own custom dog food doesn't make sense. It's too expensive and also too risky—without fine-tuned control over the balance of nutrients, you may add too much of this, too little of that. By adding too much bone meal or zinc, for example, you may actually cause harm. High-quality commercial feeds, especially those designed for working dogs, are nutritionally complete and balanced.

If you choose a commercial feed, make sure the ration contains everything the dog needs. A premium commercial feed probably does not need supplementation. You may want to try out a few different brands to see what feed works best for your dog. A shiny, clean-feeling coat is a surefire sign of proper nutrition. If the dog's coat is dry, flaky, or feels dirty, or the ends of the hair split or turn red, that's a sign that something is wrong. The problem may be a poor-quality feed or parasitic worms.

Small, firm, dark stools are a good sign of high digestibility. Give your dog time to adjust to any new diet before you begin evaluating the end results (so to speak) of that diet. Some feeds will produce small, firm stools right away; others may take a few weeks.

Whether or not to soak commercial dry feed in water is a subject of ongoing debate. Those of us who own dogs that are accustomed to eating soaked food are generally wary of feeding dry kibble. Sled dogs are not known for finesse at the supper table, and a hungry husky may bolt down dry dog food without chewing a single bite. As those kibbles go down the gullet basically intact, the dog often hacks and coughs or hunches his stomach up with what appears to be discomfort. Sometimes the entire meal is vomited back up. Also, there may be more danger of bloat and possibly torsion (a twisted stomach) with a dry, unsoaked feed because it soaks up water in the dog's digestive tract and can block the stomach or intestines. By soaking the feed, you allow it to swell up outside the digestive tract, and you get that much more water into the dog. Too much water is not necessarily recommended, however. Adding enough water to thoroughly soak the feed without turning it into soup is an effective compromise. Many dog drivers feed dry kibble with water poured over it just before serving, and that also seems to work well.

For snacking purposes, chunks of meat, dog-food kibbles, or commercial dog treats all work well. Fat can also be used as a snack. If you use meat, lamb makes a good snack after a run and is a source of fat. Liver is another popular choice. A lot of liver will cause the stool to become black, which can also be a sign of losing blood, so keep track of the amount of liver you feed. Be careful to monitor the dog's weight closely. Fat in particular can put too much weight on a dog in no time at all. A dog biscuit is a fine reward at the end of a short run, but longer runs will require some sort of recovery drink and a heftier snack to recharge the dog's energy stores.

In the summer, it's important to keep your dog well muscled and well maintained. If at all possible, keep him on the same brand of dog food you use during the winter but feed smaller amounts. Some people switch to a "lower-octane" version (lower percentages of protein and fat) of the same brand, if such is available. Don't sacrifice quality, however. The principle here is analogous to a human athlete who eats well in the winter but then changes to a diet of potato chips and soda in the summer. It will take that athlete a lot longer to get back in shape come fall than one who continues to eat a well-balanced diet all summer long.

Off-season snacks don't need to be liver or other high-octane items. In fact, summer snacks and feeds with lower protein levels seem to keep the dogs from becoming too hyper in the off season.

Mari's Winter Feeding Regime

In average amounts per dog:
- Morning: five cups baited water
- Evening: four cups feed (mixture of premium meat and kibble) with two cups water poured over it

Carol's Winter Feeding Regime

In average amounts per dog:
- Morning: four cups baited water
- Evening: approximately two cups commercial dog food (32 percent protein, 20 percent fat), soaked in water

Water

Water is a vitally important element of your dog's diet. A well-hydrated dog is healthier than one that has insufficient water in its diet. During the winter months, your dog should drink at least one to one and a half quarts of water per day, not counting the liquid in feed soaked with water. A0 mere 3 percent level of dehydration will cause a 20 percent loss of performance, so adequate water is essential. Mari waits for two to three hours after she waters her dogs before she runs them. If you usually water your dogs in the morning but run them later in the day, you may want to give them a small drink about a half hour before you run them to keep them from dipping snow.

The water you give your dogs in the winter can be quite warm, but be careful not to get it too hot. If you have a persnickety dog that refuses to drink too-warm water, often a handful of snow will cool that dog's water to a more acceptable temperature. Some dogs tip over their water dishes if the water is too hot, a habit you

A recycled plastic container makes a handy water bowl at a race. In the dog yard, stainless steel is a better choice.

don't want to encourage. It's a difficult habit to break, particularly because if you say "No!" when the dog starts to tip over the dish, sometimes that dog will decide you are telling her not to drink!

A couple of tricks for dish dumpers may help: One is to pet and praise the dog while you dole out her breakfast. Another is to put a smaller amount in the bowl, then come back and add more later. Yet another trick is to take the bowl away immediately if the dog doesn't dive into it. After a couple of days of going without, the dog soon learns to eat and drink as soon as she is served. If your dogs won't drink clear water, you can bait it with a small amount of feed, scraps, or broth to encourage the dogs to drink and also to give them an added boost of nutrients. Conversely, if your dog is used to baited water but is sick, he may prefer to drink clear water until he feels better.

Many dog drivers give their dogs baited water in the morning and feed the main meal at night. You can either mix water in with the food and let the food soak up the water, pour water over the food as you feed it, or give the dogs a little water right after eating. Some dogs will drink clear or baited water if it's offered immediately after feeding, but not if it's offered more than a half hour after. When you're traveling with dogs, it's logistically easier to give them food and water all at once early in the evening, so that you don't have to let your dogs out to relieve themselves in the middle of the night.

Small-Kennel Management
Dogs and Kids

If you acquire several dogs, and particularly if you keep them in a dog yard, you need to be extremely careful about the combination of dogs and children. Young children have been severely hurt or even killed because they wandered into a dog yard.

When you put multiple dogs on chains or in a pen in a dog yard, several factors make that yard potentially dangerous for children.

The dogs are effectively in a pack and may exhibit pack behavior. They may become more aggressive, more protective, or simply more excitable because they egg each other on. A dog that is perfectly safe on its own may become dangerous when it is in a dog yard with several other agitated dogs. If a child falls down and starts screaming, the canine predatory instinct may kick in and the dog may attack the child as if it were prey. Also, a dog's tie-out chain can cause severe injury if a child gets tangled in it when a dog is jumping around.

If you have children in your neighborhood, your best bet is to enclose your dog yard with a large chain-link fence and make sure the gate closure is out of reach of a young child or even padlocked. Talk to your neighbors and ask parents to teach their children never to approach strange dogs or enter a dog yard. Teaching children about dogs, closer parental supervision, or better dog-yard enclosures could have prevented virtually all the tragedies we've heard of involving sled dogs and children.

Enclosures

Enclosing your dog yard is generally a good idea; even if stray kids are not a problem, stray dogs can be. A fence also comes in handy if one of your chained dogs gets loose. If you have unspayed females, they should be separated from the males and should be fenced in either year-round or at least when they're in heat. Even if your own males are tied up, a stray male could breed with your female if she's not safely penned. Accidental breedings happen even in the best kennels. Please avoid adding to the overpopulation of unwanted pups.

Feeding and Watering Multiple Dogs

If you have one or two dogs, it's a simple matter to fill each dog's food bowl and hand the bowls out individually. But what if you have five or six dogs? Try balancing six bowls in your hands while you attempt to navigate past hungry, excited dogs. One simple alternative is to mix all the food in a large bucket, then ladle out individual portions with an industrial-size ladle or scoop. The same tip applies to watering with baited water in the winter. You can soak a little dog food in a bucket full of warm water, then ladle out each dog's portion.

Most sled dogs will polish their feed dishes until they shine, but if any of your dogs doesn't routinely clean his own dish, be sure to wash it regularly. It's a good idea to occasionally sterilize food dishes either in a dishwasher or in boiling water. Don't forget to wash the feed bucket and ladle every night to prevent food poisoning, especially if you use meat or soak your feed.

Proper storage is important if you purchase large quantities of feed at a time. Some dog foods will go rancid or become moldy if kept in a hot or moist environment. Meat is especially tricky to store. Even when frozen, large temperature variations can cause problems. If you find all your dogs coming down with the "flu," make sure your problem isn't actually feed management.

Transporting Several Dogs

The ease of carrying one or two dogs and a pair of skis in the back of your car is one of the great attractions of skijoring. But occasionally, the skijorer can be bitten by the "dog-acquiring bug." Carol started out with her house dog and a pair of skis. She ended up with a kennel of fourteen dogs, a dog hauler, two sleds, a second pair of skis, and...well, you get the idea.

If you have several dogs, you may want to consider buying or building a dog hauler, also known as "dog boxes." A dog hauler usually is designed to sit on the back of a pickup truck and has individual compartments for the dogs. The individual dog boxes provide each dog with a safe, sheltered place to ride. They are usually fairly snug so that the dog won't get thrown about on rough roads and so he can warm his box with body heat. A layer of bedding straw or hay gives him a warmer, more comfortable ride.

If you have just a few dogs, consider transporting them in airline kennels (also known as sky kennels) in your car to keep them out of trouble and to provide more safety for them in an accident. If you travel long distances, be sure to exercise the dogs daily and try to keep them on a regular feeding schedule.

Caring for and maintaining several working dogs can be a challenge, but it seems there are always new time-saving ideas and tips being passed around dog-driving circles. If you find yourself with more than one or two dogs, going to dog-mushing races or visiting a dog musher's kennel may provide you with several good maintenance techniques. Ideally, you should make the rounds of several mushing kennels, from small to gigantic, keeping your eyes

The boxes on this dog hauler have expanded steel screens on the doors to provide ventilation and to keep excited dogs from digging their way out. Eyebolts around the vehicle's frame provide a convenient place to clip drop chains. Dog haulers are designed to transport multiple dogs in safety, warmth, and security.

and ears open the whole time. Don't forget the potential wealth of knowledge among purebred kennels as well.

Physical Care

Conscientious dog care saves you time, money, and peace of mind all the way around. You will feed your dogs less if you keep them warm and you will get peak performance with less effort if you pay close attention to each dog's physical needs.

Feet

Obviously, your dog isn't much good without his feet, yet it is surprising how many skijorers completely neglect their dogs' feet. If your dog doesn't have healthy feet, don't expect much dog power.

Toenails that are too long reduce the dog's traction on hard or icy surfaces and are more prone to splitting and breaking. Your dog will run faster and more comfortably with well-trimmed toenails. In the wintertime, you may have to clip toenails as often as twice a month because they don't wear down fast in the snow.

If your dog has extremely long toenails, you won't be able to cut them as short as you'd like because the quick (the pinkish-red

DAVE PARTEE

vein within the nail) grows longer along with the toenail. If you clip the ends of the toenails weekly—carefully avoiding the quick—until you work them down to a reasonable length, the quick will gradually recede.

Ideally, check your dog's feet every day in the winter, or at least after every run. Examine the pads for cracks and check under the toenails for sores. Spread the foot out and inspect the webbing in between the pads. This is particularly important in dry snow conditions. A fissure in the webbing can develop as a result of sharp snow crystals or snowballs between the pads, and it will need attention to heal.

If you stay on top of foot problems with ointment and booties, you can avoid serious foot injuries. Choose an ointment that is not water soluble. Some baby ointments work well. Veterinarians sometimes carry foot ointments that have both oils and antibiotics. You may need to bootie an injured foot to keep it dry. Dry feet heal more quickly, but a bad split can take about two weeks to heal completely, even if the dog is laid off.

On the trail, if the snow is soft or wet, or if the dog suddenly starts performing poorly, stop and check his feet. He may have picked up snowballs that make it painful to run. Certain breeds seem to have more problems with snowballs, particularly dogs with long, fine hair. If a dog is known to have bad feet, it may help to clip the hair between the pads. Ointment can help keep the pads soft, especially in cold weather. It may also be necessary to bootie a dog with bad feet, but always take them off after a run.

Be careful how tightly you put on the booties. They fall off right away if they're too loose, but if they're too tight, they can cut off circulation to the foot. Getting the right fit comes with practice. Booties also tend to rub on a dog's dewclaws. Removing the dewclaws when a pup is just a few days old makes a world of difference if she has to wear booties fairly often when she grows up. Ask your veterinarian for more information on how to remove them as painlessly and safely as possible.

Ears

Make sure the dog's ears are clean and periodically check for infections. If a dog shakes his head a lot, scratches excessively at his ears, or moans when you massage his ears, that can be a sign of infection. Floppy-eared dogs seem to be more prone to moisture-related infection than those with perked ears.

Coat

A healthy dog's coat should feel clean and soft, rather than dry, oily, or dirty. If a dog's coat is dry, red, or split, it may indicate worms or a nutritional deficiency that should be checked out. If your dog is healthy but has a mediocre coat, you may be able to improve the coat by switching to a different dog food or by supplementing with fat.

Some dog breeds require regular brushing or combing to keep the coat clean and to prevent matting. Others, huskies in particular, need little grooming—they have medium-length, coarse guard hairs that resist tangling and matting. But even low-maintenance huskies should be groomed when they shed their winter coats. The coat itches a lot as it "blows," and the dog will be more comfortable if that dead hair is combed out. A medium- or wide-toothed dog comb works well on the dense undercoat of huskies and other coarse-coated dogs.

Some people like to think their dogs are too "tough" to need grooming, even during shedding season. But besides making your dog more comfortable, grooming makes him look healthy and well cared for.

Weight

How do you tell if a dog is too fat or too thin? When you run your hands over a dog of optimum working weight (which differs considerably from what's considered a good show weight), you should be able to feel the ribs. You also should be able to feel the hip bones, but the flesh should be level between the bones and you should be able to feel a small padding of fat over the spine between the hip bones.

Pet dog owners seem more likely to err on the side of too much weight than too little. But you do your dog no favors by making her cart around excess pounds. Here's an analogy: What does it feel like to run a mile when you are ten pounds overweight? You work harder, your heart beats harder, you lose your breath more quickly, and your muscles become much more sore. You're not being cruel to your dog when you keep her trim. You're making it easier and more comfortable for her to run.

If you are not comfortable judging your dog's weight for yourself, ask to visit a reputable dog-mushing kennel. Those dogs might look too skinny to you, but they are usually at the ideal weight for

DAVE PARTEE

Proper weight is important for working dogs. You don't want your dog so thin that she uses all her energy for physiological maintenance, yet she shouldn't haul around extra pounds, either. If kept at optimum weight, these dogs will live longer, work better, and be happier and healthier in the long run.

sound health and peak performance. Your veterinarian is another source of feedback. Be sure to tell the veterinarian beforehand that this is a working dog, not a show or pet dog. If possible, ask a veterinarian who is familiar with sled dogs.

Because the dog is an athlete, his weight is important even in the summertime. Keeping down a dog's weight in the heat of summer will help him stay a little cooler. In the winter, maintaining proper weight becomes essential. Some mushers like to keep their dogs just a bit heavier than racing weight in the fall, because the dogs are building up muscle as well as increasing their available energy. This is also why it's important to give the dogs warm, dry shelter, so they don't have to use as much of their food energy to stay warm in the rain or snow.

Vaccinations, Worming, and Preventive Medicine

Dogs should be vaccinated regularly, beginning when they are pups and continuing throughout their life as recommended by a veterinarian. If you acquire a pup that's eight to twelve weeks old when you take it from the litter, make sure it is friendly, curious and healthy looking. Ask the breeder if the pup has been wormed and vaccinated. It's a good idea to take any new dog to the veterinarian to have it checked for general health. An infected pup or adult dog may bring diseases or parasites home to your kennel.

Canine vaccinations include rabies, distemper, parvo, corona, and sometimes other diseases such as kennel cough. Check with your veterinarian for an appropriate vaccination schedule. Rabies shots are usually effective for two or three years, and state law customarily mandates frequency. Competitive dog drivers tend to give vaccinations in the fall, so that they are most potent during the racing season.

It's important to worm your dog regularly. If you have just a few dogs, your best course of action may be to bring fecal samples to your veterinarian and have them tested for worms. Owners of large kennels don't always test for worms (too expensive!); they simply worm their dogs regularly as a matter of course. However, even large kennels can benefit from testing a few dogs to make sure their worming program is doing the job.

Mari worms her dogs at least four times a year; Carol worms twice a year—once in the spring and once in the fall. You should rotate worming medicines to increase their overall effectiveness. Ask your veterinarian to put you on a regular schedule of different wormers. Mari believes in also treating dogs for coccidiosis, beginning as pups.

If you know your dogs have an infectious disease, don't bring them to a public trail, as a favor to other dog drivers who may train on those trails. On the other hand, be aware that you are almost guaranteed to infect your dogs with something if you yourself train on public trails. It seems as if kennels go through some kind of virus every fall just the way kids who are returning to school catch colds and the flu. It may take a week or two for the dogs to recover. This strengthens the case for cleaning up after your dogs whenever you go to a public trail. Always carry a shovel and poop bucket or other container. Worms in particular are often transmitted when a dog sniffs a wormy dog's stools. However, don't worry excessively about public trails. You want your dogs to become immune to diseases, and if you never take your dogs to a public trail, they will never develop the antibodies they need to combat local "bugs."

When it comes to clinical care of your dog, it's important to choose a veterinarian you feel comfortable working with. We are lucky in Alaska because most of our veterinarians know a lot about sled dogs and working dogs in general. Elsewhere, it may be harder to find a veterinarian who is familiar with skijoring or dog mushing. A veterinarian who works with hunting dogs or working dogs in general may be more familiar with the types of injuries a skijoring dog is prone to.

If you are moving into a new area, make preliminary appointments with a couple of different veterinarians to see if they have time to talk to you and if they seem interested in skijoring or dog mushing. It may be best to find two or three different veterinarians or clinics that you can work with. A second opinion might come in handy for difficult injuries or a tenacious flu bug. You may also find that one clinic will carry a particular medication that another clinic doesn't.

Neutering

Neutering used to be a touchy subject, but it has become more and more commonplace for dog drivers to neuter dogs they don't intend to breed. Folklore had it that neutering a working dog reduced its

DAVE PARTEE

This competitive skijorer has won numerous races in the skijoring, four-dog, and six-dog classes in Fairbanks. She neuters all of her dogs yet has seen no reduction in their drive or speed.

speed and drive, but most of us who neuter our dogs have found that to be false.

Neutering has several significant benefits. A neutered male is far less likely to fight or exhibit excessively dominant behavior. Neutering females eliminates the possibility of accidental breeding, keeps strange male dogs out of your yard, and can alleviate the hormonal difficulties some female dogs experience when they are in season. Both sexes are less prone to certain diseases later in life if neutered early. Neutering also reduces the terrible waste of unwanted puppies that end up at the animal shelter.

Several competitive dog mushers have evaluated the speed and drive of neutered dogs and have found little or no reduction in ability or attitude. The worst "drawback" to neutering—that the dog may gain weight more easily—is not a drawback at all. It simply means you need to feed smaller amounts, which makes the dog cheaper to maintain. The cost of neutering can appear prohibitive if you own several dogs, but this one-time expense has positive benefits that last for a lifetime.

Injuries and Ailments

Kathy Frost, an Alaskan sprint-mushing champion for many years, had a maxim she liked to tell new dog drivers: "If your best dog suddenly turns bad, he doesn't need discipline. He needs veterinary care." If a dog that has been doing well suddenly starts acting unhappy or won't pull, it's almost always a medical problem. After having heard Kathy say this many times, Carol experienced it firsthand when her steadiest and most enthusiastic puller, Sugar, began to perform poorly. Physical inspections turned up nothing obvious—no swollen joints, no foot injuries, no limp, and no apparent illness. If Carol hadn't known the dog well, she might have decided Sugar was just slacking off, but Sugar had never before been a discipline problem for her.

Carol began to notice a subtle overall stiffness in Sugar that steadily worsened. Giving the dog a rest didn't help the stiffness.

At last, Kathy herself solved the mystery: Sugar was likely suffering from hypothyroidism, a trait that ran in her bloodline. Thyroid supplements brought a dramatic improvement, and Sugar was back to her old bouncy self within a week.

If you suspect a problem, go through the basics first: Inspect the feet, check the ears, and see if the mouth is dry or the gums white (white gums can signify dehydration or anemia). You may want to bring in a stool sample to be tested for parasites. If your dog isn't stretching out, it may be a bladder or kidney infection (or in Sugar's case, low thyroid). A female dog that is just coming into heat may have cramps.

Sometimes a dog will stop performing because she is sore from falling in a moose hole or running on an icy trail. Not all injuries will result in a noticeable limp. Sometimes a sore back or pulled stomach muscle will result in a shorter, choppy gait but no limp. If you're not sure whether your dog is injured, call your veterinarian and describe the problem. The phone call only takes a few minutes, but it's good insurance against making an error in judgment.

Spotting injuries comes with experience and practice. Learn how to read your dog's *healthy* gait so you can tell when something deviates from normal. If at all possible, observe your dog while she is running loose, so that you know what her most natural gait looks like. This knowledge gives you a baseline from which to evaluate future injuries. Watch how your dog places her feet and how she stretches out.

Mari had a border collie/sled dog cross with a noticeably shorter gait than her other dogs, but she watched him carefully and knew that was his regular gait. Carol's first lead dog, Shiner, was locally renowned for his absurdly crooked gait (as well as his offbeat personality). The first time Carol saw the dog, she actually thought he was crippled, and those who ran him always remarked on the way his feet flew every which way. But that was normal—for Shiner.

If a long-gaited dog suddenly shortens up, that may be a sign of a sore shoulder or a pulled muscle in the dog's back or belly. If

DAVE PARTEE

If your dog is in the mood for play after a run, it's a good bet he's feeling fine. If he seems depressed or is unusually subdued, look carefully for soreness or injury.

you suspect a dog is injured, watch him very carefully while he is running, or have another person walk the dog while you watch his gait. Look at each shoulder and each hip to see if the dog is avoiding putting weight on that area. Pick up and bend the leg in question to see if normal movement causes discomfort.

Sometimes rest alone can treat a simple strain. To bring an injured dog back into shape, you might want to start by walking him around and gradually work him back into pulling.

Always keep a close eye on your dog's general health and work closely with your veterinarian whenever problems arise. (It's possible, however, to overdo this and continually take your dog in to the clinic for nothing. The clinic may love the extra income, but it will cost you big bucks and will eventually burn out your veterinarian.) For more specific information on common injuries and ailments, you may want to pick up books on dog care and basic veterinary procedures for the dog owner.

8

Choosing a Skijoring Dog

A Few Words About Dog Breeds

There are hundreds of recognized breeds of dogs in the world. This diversity within the species is a tribute both to canines and to the many generations of humans who have directed the dog's genetic makeup to suit our varied purposes. Volumes of information are available on specific breeds. We encourage you to read books and magazines, talk to breeders, and query other dog owners.

In the United States, the American Kennel Club is the major organization that promotes and tracks the lineage of purebred dogs. Within the AKC, a specific group of breeds is defined as working dogs. In this book, our definition of a working dog is practical rather than breed specific. To us, working dogs are dogs that have a physical job—be it herding, hunting, pulling, packing, or guarding. Most of these dogs are physically capable of being trained for skijoring. The choice of a specific breed should depend on your personality and your skijoring goals.

Beyond the host of purebred dogs, there are hundreds of canines of mixed lineage that are also perfectly capable of becoming excellent skijoring partners. And there's always the Alaskan husky, which although not recognized by the AKC, has been genetically selected and bred for its natural pulling ability.

But remember, there are exceptions to every rule. There are bird dogs that don't fetch or point, border collies that don't pay attention or herd, and sled dogs that don't pull. Choosing a specific breed simply lessens your chances of being surprised.

Before You Add a Working Dog to Your Life

If you have never owned a dog before, or if you have owned pet dogs but now are thinking of acquiring a working dog or even expanding into a bona fide kennel, it is a good idea to examine your lifestyle, your goals and desires, and the rules and regulations governing your home area. Some people are not in a position to make the kind of commitment required to own a dog, whether because of restrictions on their living situation or because their lifestyle is incompatible with dog ownership. If you are not in a position to own a skijoring dog, you might try offering some of your time to someone who has a small kennel, in return for the use of one of their dogs.

Keep in mind that a working dog has different requirements than a pet has. Some dog owners do just fine with a low-maintenance house dog but find themselves uncomfortable with the extra responsibility of a working dog. Some breeds don't adapt well to a life of boredom and will cause no end of trouble if they don't get the attention or responsibility they need. For the sake of your sanity and in fairness to the dog, don't keep a dog if you can't keep it well.

Working and living with a skijoring dog requires patience, time, commitment, the ability to train, suitable zoning and covenants, and adequate accommodations. All of these elements are relative, of course: The amount of patience required to keep a mellow, easy-going house dog that likes to pull, for example, will be far less than that required for a high-strung, obsessive working dog that *must* have a job to be happy.

Zoning and Covenants

Before any other considerations, it's a good idea to make sure you are legally allowed to keep a dog or dogs at your physical location. The zoning regulations in your area may limit the number of dogs you can keep outside or may require you to obtain a special kennel permit. Zoning usually isn't an issue if your dog or dogs live in the house, although covenants sometimes can restrict what zoning does not. Some covenants dictate the manner in which a dog can be kept or prohibit dog ownership altogether. A little advance research can save a lot of heartache. Your city, county, or borough offices should be able to tell you your zoning requirements and/ or covenants.

Keep in mind that restrictive zoning and covenants often arise as a direct result of negative experiences. Someone who has lived next to a kennel of noisy, unruly dogs is much more likely to support zoning laws and covenants that limit or ban outdoor dogs or kennels. It's simple cause and effect: Irresponsible dog ownership leads to negative public opinion, which leads to more restrictive laws. Please be considerate of your neighbors, no matter what your zoning law says.

Location

The physical character of your home has a significant impact on the type of dog that is best for you. If you live in an apartment, you might not want to keep a large dog or one that needs lots of room to run. If you have a small yard, you will probably want to keep your dog or dogs inside. Perhaps you have enough room to keep your dogs outside, but your lot is close to the neighbor's house. An eight- or nine-foot-high privacy fence around the dog yard might provide adequate separation.

For the serious skijorer, the availability of trails can be a consideration. There's nothing quite as satisfying as being able to run your dogs on trails that connect with your yard. But, as we've already said, the beauty of skijoring is that a pair of skis and a couple of dogs are eminently transportable.

Commitment

Owning a dog requires a level of commitment that some are reluctant to make. Your dog will need a comfortable place to live, regular and adequate meals, exercise, and medical attention. You will have to arrange for dog sitting whenever you'll be gone for extended periods. This commitment can last for fifteen years or more.

Patience

Do you have the patience to work with and take care of a dog or dogs? That may be a difficult question to answer. Here are some things to consider: Are you easily frustrated or angered? Do you lose your temper quickly? Are you irritated by change or by upset schedules? Owning a dog can be a bit like raising children, although the analogy is by no means perfect. We know of one dedicated dog person who is determined never to have children!

If you are impatient by nature, that doesn't necessarily mean you should never own a dog. In fact, it may well be that the dog teaches you a degree of patience you never thought possible. But it's important, we think, to go into dog ownership with the idea that patience is an absolute necessity, and that if it is not inherent in the dog owner, it will have to be acquired. Dogs are not people: you can't blow up at a dog and apologize later. Temper tantrums followed by sheepish remorse will only create confusion, mistrust, and, very likely, further misbehavior.

Time

Working with and caring for a dog takes time. If you're accustomed to twelve-hour work shifts and hectic weekends, do you really want to add a dog to the workload? If you will be pressed for time, choose a dog that doesn't require large amounts of training to learn the type of behavior you're looking for.

Training Ability

Just as some people were never meant to be parents, some were never meant to be dog trainers. Training requires common sense, consistency, a methodical progression of lessons, discipline, an affinity for the animal, and, as we mentioned before, an abundance of patience. You can't enlighten a confused dog by lengthy verbal dissertations. If the dog doesn't understand a training technique, you have to have the patience to repeat it—over and over again, if necessary—and the ability to modify the technique or break the problem down into simpler parts that the dog can understand.

Different dogs require different levels or styles of training. Take this into consideration when choosing your dog. Effective training techniques can be learned, and as we said in chapter 4, dog obedience classes are a great way to get started. Training ability is not a static skill. Good trainers keep learning all the time. Know-it-all disease seems to strike almost everyone at some point in his or her development as a trainer and dog driver, but the best trainers recuperate with a greater sense of humility and an even stronger desire to keep learning.

Responsible Dog Ownership

There is a direct cause-and-effect relationship between irresponsible dog ownership and restrictive dog ownership laws. If you feel your dog should be allowed to run loose, to bark incessantly, to roam the neighborhood at all hours, to defecate wherever it wants, and to chase whatever runs away from it, that's fine—if you live in a cabin in the wilderness and your nearest neighbor is fifty miles away. However, if your neighbors are within hearing and seeing distance of your dog, keep in mind that they have rights as well. Their rights include the right to sleep at night, the right to relatively peaceful surroundings, the right to let their kids play in the yard without being harassed or frightened by your dog, the right to drive their car down the street without being chased and without fear of hitting your dog, the right to leave a package or a garbage bag on their porch without fear of your dog stealing it, and the right to a relatively sanitary environment.

Perhaps you feel it is cruel to keep a dog on a chain. If you feel your dog has the "right" to run free, you have several choices: you can fence your yard, you can drive to an uninhabited area to let your dog loose, or you can train your dog to stay in your yard. But keep in mind that your dog does not have the right to infringe on the rights of your neighbors.

Owning a skijoring dog adds to your responsibility, but skijoring also enhances the dog-owner relationship and adds a dimension of teamwork that we feel makes it more than worth the extra

DAVE PARTEE

effort. Actually working with a dog, rather than just living with one, can create a rich level of communication and a powerful bond that can be extremely satisfying.

Choosing a Dog Breed for Skijoring

Almost any breed of dog that weighs more than about thirty pounds can pull you on skis. Even the average couch potato pet can excel at skijoring, given proper training and a basic desire to pull. Some breeds do take to pulling more easily—or more fanatically—than others, however. A breed of dog that shines in recreational work may not have the competitive edge for serious racing. If you already have a dog, the best way to save you and your dog a lot of heartache is to tailor your skijoring style to your dog's capabilities. But if you're in the market for a new dog, your choice of dog breeds—or general dog types and characteristics—can be a key factor in your success at the type of skijoring you choose.

If you're interested in recreational skijoring, consider adopting a dog from the local animal shelter. In Fairbanks, many top-notch competitive skijoring dogs and wonderful recreational skijoring dogs have come from the local shelter. A shelter dog may be perfect for your needs, and you'll have done both the animal and your community a service.

Before you research particular breeds of dog, look at the elements of your skijoring plans so that you can figure out how a given breed of dog will mesh with your expectations. To illustrate this, we've broken down the two major categories of skijoring—recreational and competitive—into a series of sample questions. Some questions are relevant to both styles.

For Recreational Skijoring

- How much do you weigh?
- Do you plan to camp overnight with your dog?
- Will your dog be expected to pull a pulk loaded with gear?

DAVE PARTEE

Working dogs who get bored and make up their own jobs sometimes find themselves at the animal shelter. Channeling that energy into skijoring can turn a problem into an asset. Two of these three hard-charging dogs are shelter dogs.

- How strong a skier are you?
- Will the terrain you skijor on be hilly or flat? Easy or difficult?
- Is your main skijoring trail in a densely populated area?
- Do you plan to travel long distances?
- Do your plans include children?
- Will your dog be expected to be a pet and companion as well as a working dog?

For Competitive Skijoring

- What are your racing goals? Are you racing for fun or to take first place?
- What distances will you be racing?
- Will the trails you ski on be well groomed, or will they be soft and snowy?
- Will you be camping overnight as part of the race?
- Do you plan to ski aggressively behind your dog, or will the dog be doing most of the work?
- What type of terrain does the racing trail cover?
- How agile a skier are you?
- How many dogs will you race with?
- Will you be racing in Nordic-style competitions (also called "pulk races" or "pulka races")?

This is not meant as a complete list of questions to be considered, but use it as a starting point. Your answers will give you important clues to some of the characteristics your new dog should have. A recreational skijorer who plans to do a lot of winter camping may want a larger dog that can pull a pulk full of camping gear. Depending on the average temperature of that skijorer's camping grounds, the dog may need a thick, warm coat as well, or may need to be well behaved enough to sleep in the tent. A light-boned, short-coated dog would be less appropriate in this situation, but might be fine for day trips or milder climates.

If the same skijorer is a powerful skier who camps light, and the terrain is primarily flat, the size of the dog becomes less important. A smaller dog with good endurance might work out just as well as a larger one. A young skijorer or a person with marginal skiing ability may want to put more emphasis on a levelheaded, people-oriented breed. For this person, strength or endurance may be secondary to trainability and personality.

A competitive skijorer's answers may indicate the need for a lightning-fast dog, with size less relevant and speed, endurance, and drive all-important. If your racing trails are usually set in soft, wet snow, a dog with good feet is important. An aggressive skier can race with a smaller dog than a skier who depends on the dog to do the bulk of the work. Long-distance races require a stronger emphasis on endurance, and Nordic-style competitions (where the dog pulls a pulk) require a dog with adequate strength to pull the extra load.

Almost any dog, from a Saint Bernard to a Brittany spaniel, can be an enjoyable skijoring partner. Size is usually less of an issue than personality, attitude, and trainability. The best partnerships come from mutual trust and taking pleasure in working with each other.

Once you have developed a list of characteristics you would like in a dog, the next step is to see how various dog breeds measure up to your requirements. In our experience, some dog breeds are better for racing, others for recreation, and some are better than others for different tasks within those two main categories. You may want to gather information on specific breeds and make a chart of their "scores" in such categories as pulling instinct, speed, strength, levelheadedness, coat, feet, people-orientation, endurance, and trainability.

Keep in mind that different bloodlines of a particular breed and individual dogs within each breed can vary greatly from "average." Talk to owners of the breeds you are interested in, talk to other skijorers, talk to dog mushers, and talk to professional dog breeders. Remember, only you will have to live with your choice, so ignore any advice that doesn't fit you personally. Beware of breed fanatics who may make claims for their breed based on love and admiration rather than hard, cold evidence. If at all possible, try out the dog before you buy it. Many breeders place customer satisfaction above financial gain and will take a dog back (within a reasonable length of time) if the buyer is unhappy with the results. Some breeders actually require that the dog go back to the breeder if she doesn't work out for the buyer.

One last consideration: How well does the personality of a particular dog breed—or bloodline within a breed—mesh with your own? This question is far from frivolous. Many professional dog drivers and purebred kennel owners will tell you they've

171

emphasized a certain lineage of dog because they like the attitude or personality of that bloodline. Dog driving is a team effort, a meshing of human and canine psychology. No matter how physically suitable a given dog may be, he will not do as well for you, nor will you work as well with him, if the two of you are not compatible.

For example, perhaps you are a competitive racer with a fast, hardworking dog, but that same dog drives you crazy by constantly screaming and leaping in harness. By the time you get out on the trail, you're tired and your temper is frayed. Or you have a dog that runs just fine but is timid and spooky around you—and you don't like shy dogs. Perhaps you're gentle and soft-spoken, but your dog is hard-headed and deaf to lower decibels. Or maybe you have a loud, dynamic personality that intimidates your ultrasensitive, keen-eared canine teammate. These considerations can be as important as a dog's speed or strength.

Take the time to analyze what you want in a dog and research breeds that will best fit your goals. The time you spend can pay off in dividends far beyond first place in a skijoring race, or a dog that can pull your gear across miles of wilderness. Your dog is your partner—choose one you can live with.

A Buyer's Guide to Puppies

Once you've chosen a breed, do you want a puppy or an adult? A trained adult dog can save time and you can skijor with it right away instead of waiting for it to grow up. However, if you have the time and energy to start out with a pup, you can mold that pup to meet your individual needs and personality.

When you are ready to shop, look for a kennel with a reputation for high-quality dogs. Purebreds sometimes come with guarantees concerning hip dysplasia, eye problems, and other genetic defects. Alaskan huskies usually don't come with written guarantees, but some breeders will offer you an informal guarantee against any obvious physical defects that crop up after the purchase.

If you purchase a sled dog pup from a kennel that has proven bloodlines, and your pup's litter is friendly and well socialized, you have perhaps as high as an 85 to 90 percent chance that the dog will run. A pup from a kennel of top Alaskan racing sled dogs may cost several hundred dollars. The price on a purebred pup may be much higher. If you are interested in competitive skijoring or Nordic-style racing, you will be better off spending the money on proven bloodlines than taking your chances with a pup from an unknown or unproven breed.

Ask to observe an entire litter in action before you buy. Watch how the pups play. You'll usually be able to pick out the bossiest and shyest pups right away. Unless you work extremely well with spooky dogs, don't pick the pup that sits back in the corner, the one you feel sorry for. That pup may not be healthy or it may be inherently shy. The rudest, most dominant pup may not be the best choice, either. Look for a pup that comes up to you right away, seems to want to please you, and is bright-eyed and alert. For skijoring, it's particularly important to have an open-minded dog.

If you are concerned with a pup's potential dominance, those who raise dogs have a technique for determining a dog's dominance factor that they use when the pup is quite young. If you turn a tiny pup on its back in your hand and it fights a lot to get back on its feet, that indicates it is likely to be a more dominant dog than the pup that just lies there trustingly.

Mari likes a dog that's a little bit of a loner. The dog isn't too interested in people or in other dogs. They seem to have more self-confidence and at the same time are not fighters. Loner types seem to cue in more strongly to whatever they love in life. They aren't easily distracted, and they appear to think more, for some reason. Sometimes a pup will noticeably cue into you. That connection may pay off in the long run.

It's reasonable to ask to see how the pups act and run, and you can make some initial assessments based on those factors. Ask the breeder if you can take the pups for a walk. Observe their behavior—how they run, which ones want to run up front, which ones would rather stay behind you. Look for a pup that's more open-minded and wants to run ahead of you. It will likely be easier for that dog to learn the leading skills necessary for skijoring than the one who stays behind your heels.

Look at each pup's overall health, gait, and conformation. If you don't know much about conformation, bring a knowledgeable friend with you. Look at how the pup's feet are put together, how good its coat is, and its general appearance or overall "look." Ask whether the pups have been wormed regularly. (A wormy pup may be thin around the ribs, hips, and shoulders yet have a fat belly as if it has just eaten a big meal.) Make sure they've had regular vaccinations. Whether you visit a kennel of Alaskan huskies, mixed breeds, or purebreds, they all should be well taken care of.

Ultimately, you will be responsible for developing the pup into a skijoring dog, but if you have a high-quality pup to start with, you will greatly increase your chances of success.

A Buyer's Guide to Adult Dogs

Perhaps you don't have the wherewithal to deal with a pup, or you want to start skijoring this season and can't wait a year or so until the pup is old enough to pull you. Depending on your training skills, you may want to train an adult pet to skijor. The easiest way to get started in a hurry is to purchase an adult dog that is already harness trained. Be wary, however, of mushers who say, "Oh, that would make a great skijoring dog!" about one of their team dogs that has never been in front of skis in his life. You may well find that the first time you try to skijor with him, he takes one look at those weird sticks on your feet and thinks, "No way!" We've seen superlative team dogs—and even veteran lead dogs—lie down and refuse to move when asked to pull a skier. Their initial reaction often can be overcome with training, but don't necessarily expect a superlative performance the first time out.

When Mari sells a dog for skijoring out of her racing sled-dog kennel, usually she has skijored with the dog herself to make sure it will pull a skier. She then recommends that the buyer try out the dog at her kennel, on trails familiar to the dog. This requires a level of trust between the breeder and the buyer.

It's not uncommon for kennel owners to be pickier about buyers than buyers are about breeders. One of the jobs of a responsible breeder is to sell the right dog to the right person. If a breeder doesn't think a potential buyer is a competent dog person or suspects the buyer doesn't really know what he or she is doing, the breeder may call off the sale. Breeders know that if a good dog is badly handled and its performance suffers as a result, that can reflect negatively on the breeder even if it is the new owner's fault.

Be sure your expectations match the capabilities and training of the dog you intend to purchase. Here's an example of how expectations can backfire: A skijorer buys an Alaskan husky sled dog from a sprint-racing kennel. The dog has been trained in a competitive eight-dog team and is accustomed to going ten miles a day and then coming home and resting until the next day's run. The skijorer has bought the dog to use as a working dog out at his cabin, where he commonly runs the same three-mile loop several times a day. Pretty soon his new dog doesn't want to pull anymore, and the skijorer decides the dog is no good. But the problem is not with the dog. The problem is incompatible expectations. The dog is unaccustomed to going out several times a day, he's bored silly by running the same trail over and over again, and he's confused about what's expected of him. If that same skijorer gets a pup and trains it himself, that pup will likely do just fine at the same task where the other dog flunked.

Teaching your own pet to pull can give you an advantage if you plan to ask for behavior outside the normal range of a trained sled dog. Carol's first skijoring dog, Willow, and Mari's first border collie, Alex—both of them pets as well as working dogs—were what we call "bombproof." Throughout their lives, the dogs were exposed to a number of different and unusual situations. Willow could pull a series of novice skijorers up and down a parking lot several times in a row without any hesitation. Both dogs were used in videotaping sessions (with grueling "retakes") and they both appeared on television. Alex patiently worked a photo shoot that involved lots of stopping and starting with a young skijorer. But if you ask these things of a dog that has not been bombproofed, the odds are that the dog won't be able to tolerate multiple drivers, repetitive tasks, noise and bright lights, or other strange occurrences. Adult dogs aren't computers; they can't be reprogrammed in a day. Sometimes they can't be reprogrammed at all.

If you think a particular dog can meet your expectations, look carefully at your prospective purchase. Ask why the person is selling the dog. Has the dog been injured? How often? Is it not quite fast enough? Does it have trouble with the pressure of a bigger team? Is it better at short runs than at long distances? There has to be a reason the dog is for sale, and most breeders will be honest about that reason. Be a little wary if the breeder makes excuses for the dog or builds it up too much. If the breeder comes across like a car salesperson and tries to push the dog on you, you're smart to be suspicious of a sales pitch.

Try the dog out. Get a feeling for whether you like the dog or not. Look at how the dog is built. Conformation, bone structure, and muscle placement have a substantial impact on a dog's ability to pull. Make sure the dog you are considering is sound and moves freely. You may want to read a few books on dog conformation before you go shopping.

Again, this may be a good time to bring a knowledgeable friend with you. Your friend may pick up more quickly on the dog's overall gait and conformation, or may have a better comprehension of what the breeder says about the dog's good and bad points.

Basic bone structure will affect the way a dog moves and her ability to pull. No matter the breed, the dog should be physically sound.

Listen carefully to what the owner tells you. Often a shortcoming for the previous owner will prove an asset for you, or at least a less critical flaw. Perhaps you're looking at a dog from a sprint team that is ten seconds too slow over a mile. He has good feet and eats well, so he might be just great for touring or longer skijoring races. If the dog has sore feet, that may be a sufficient reason for a large-kennel owner to sell him, but it's a problem that can be dealt with in a small kennel. Maybe the dog doesn't travel well or is a bad eater when he's on the road. If you don't travel much, the same dog may work out wonderfully for you.

If you are purchasing the dog from a reputable breeder, the dog likely is well worth the purchase. The best breeders don't sell poor-quality dogs, because they know it will hurt their reputation to do so. They often refuse to sell a marginal dog out of a sense of responsibility to the dog, as well. All too often such dogs end up bouncing from owner to owner and eventually show up at the animal shelter, on the side of the road, or abandoned to starve.

Be forewarned: A team dog may not skijor as well as a lead dog, but leaders are much more expensive. You may be presented with a price of $2,000 or more for a trained gee-haw leader. If you are accustomed to the purebred market, you may not be as shocked by these dog prices, since a registered purebred dog is rarely cheap. But if you've gotten all your dogs from the local shelter, it may be difficult to see the point in paying more than $100 for a dog.

If you think the price is unreasonable, ask around first. Do some comparison shopping. But keep this in mind: the price you pay up front for a top-quality dog is a one-time expense, and it costs no more to feed and house a good dog than a bad one.

Breeding

If you already have a few good dogs in your yard, and you find you want to expand your kennel, your first impulse may be to have your own litter of pups. Please consider this prospect from all angles before you go forward. You'll be adding to an already overloaded dog population. Is it worth doing so? Are you sure you can find good homes for any pups you don't want to keep?

Are you prepared to take on the expense and responsibility? Pregnant and nursing bitches need extra food and care. Pups eat a *lot* of food because they are growing so fast. You'll need a warm, dry place for whelping and for the pups when they are young. Unless you have ten acres, no neighbors, and a puppyproof yard, you'll need a pen to keep them in when the pups are older. Loose pups get into all kinds of mischief, and your neighbors will not appreciate having their garbage ripped into or their belongings stolen by errant pups. When curious pups begin to cruise their turf, they tend to bring embarrassing odds and ends home from the house next door, and they will enthusiastically eat up, dig into, or otherwise destroy anything *you've* left lying around as well.

Pups must be vaccinated and wormed on a regular basis. You may find your litter contracting a life-threatening illness such as parvo; are you willing and ready to nurse sick puppies? Raising a litter of pups is expensive even when all goes well, and vet bills can add hundreds of dollars to the regular maintenance costs. From a financial perspective, you might save a lot of money by simply buying a pup.

Are you breeding the kind of bloodlines that will produce high-quality pups? Where did your dogs come from? If you got them from the pound or from someone who couldn't provide a pedigree, you are playing roulette with your breeding program—and it's the pups that will end up paying the price if the program doesn't work out. If you purchased your dogs from a top breeder, talk to that breeder about your plans. If the breeder is reputable (and not just interested in persuading you to buy another pup instead) and your breeding plans make sense, he or she may encourage you to go ahead with the breeding. But he may also be able to present you with information that will help you make a decision about whether to breed or not, and to whom. If you have a wonderful female dog, it might be worthwhile to pay a stud fee to breed her to a good male from compatible bloodlines. Some breeders will provide a sire or dam in return for splitting a litter with you.

Even if you feel confident about your dogs' bloodlines, there are other elements to take into consideration. If possible, look at the parents—and even the grandparents—of the dogs you have. What kind of dogs are they? Are they hard-headed or soft-headed, are they leaders, are they nicely built, do they have good feet, do they eat well? It's also important to find out if they have any inherited diseases or other negative traits. If your dog has a genetic tendency toward low thyroid or a physical defect, for example, don't breed that dog. You're just perpetuating a problem if you do.

Don't count on producing a litter of lead dogs by breeding two leaders. The genetic basis for producing lead dogs isn't that simple. Sometimes it takes several different breedings to discover that a dog produces leaders.

Look at the attitudes of the dogs you plan to breed. Some breeders go for live-wire screamers; others prefer a calmer attitude. One breeder may focus on hard-headed, solid types, while another may work better with dogs that have softer traits. Choosing a dog for its attitude is not unusual among dog drivers, and in skijoring, it's especially important to have a dog that will listen to you. Training can go a long way toward developing that, of course, but focusing on traits compatible with your training style will increase your chances of being happy with the outcome of your breeding.

Blending attitudes can work well. Breeding a mellow, almost sour-acting dog to one that's lively and excited may produce a dog with a better mix of attitude and levelheadedness. Ironically, breeding for intelligence can backfire—a dog that is too smart may get bored with running or may become devious and manipulative. (It has been said that part of the reason for mixing hound blood in with husky blood was to soften the intelligence and canniness of the husky. A full-blooded husky, with its strong survival instincts, might see no reason to keep going once it got tired, whereas a hound would tend to go until it dropped.)

All in all, breeding is no simple matter, and mistakes can mean yet more unwanted pups at the shelter, or adult dogs who get passed around because they never quite make the grade. If you're still considering breeding, please avoid breeding females indiscriminately. An overpopulation of mediocre puppies decreases their individual value, and free pups or those that end up at the shelter have less value than those that have good bloodlines and cost money. Dogs are not assembly-line products. They are living, sentient beings. It is a terrible waste to destroy tens of thousands of unwanted dogs because of irresponsible breeding—which is precisely the situation

The breed of dog you already own can be the best choice of all—and looking adorable in a dog coat is just a bonus.

across the United States today. Careful and judicious breeding is not just more economical but more ethical as well.

Puppy Raising

If you do breed, or if you acquire a whole litter of pups that someone else has bred, here are a few suggestions for raising them.

Mari likes to keep nursing mothers in a pen until the pups are about three to four weeks old. She then lets the pups run loose or moves mother and pups into a large pen, because the pups seem to become friendlier that way. Ideally, she lets the pups run loose around her yard, but when she had young children, that was not feasible. Mari has found that if you try to put free-running pups back in a pen after they are three to four months old, they will fight it and try to climb out. However, if you pen the pups at night from the beginning, they will become accustomed to being confined. In other words, either get your pups used to the pen right away or leave them loose until they are old enough to be chained out. For some reason, some lines of sled dogs seem to adjust better to chains than to pens. Apparently, pens make them feel more restricted and isolated than chains do. But if they are used to pens from an early age, they accept them more readily later on.

We've also found that if you begin chaining up a pup as soon as it is old enough (about three to four months), it learns to accept the chain relatively quickly and easily. Some people don't want to confine a dog until they absolutely have to, so they wait until the

DAVE PARTEE

dog is a year old before they first chain it up. But our experience has been that the older a dog is, the harder it becomes for that dog to accept restrictions on its freedom. A year-old dog may fight and howl and bark incessantly on its new chain, and this argument may continue long after a young pup would accept the situation. It seems much kinder to teach a three- or four-month-old pup, even though it will still complain for a while. Leash training at about eight to ten weeks old will help facilitate chain training at three to four months.

Teaching a pup to accept a chain is a little like teaching a child to sleep in its own bed instead of yours. If you keep relenting by letting the pup off its chain when it makes a fuss, the pup learns that howling will get results. In effect, the pup is training you! But if you draw firm boundaries, the pup will soon adjust.

Also take another look at the puppy socialization techniques back in chapter 4 in the section on teaching a pup to skijor. Exposing your pups to a variety of objects and new experiences when they are young will help them develop into confident, open-minded adult dogs. Children are great for socializing puppies, and the children learn to be gentle and loving toward animals at the same time.

9

Nordic-Style
Dog Mushing

Nordic-style dog mushing is the sport of skijoring behind a small sled, a pulk, pulled by one to three dogs. This variety of dog driving may be a novelty in the United States, but the first Nordic-style dog-mushing club in Norway started in the early 1930s. Nordic-style races there have been held for many decades, and until fairly recently, Nordic-style races in Europe outnumbered Alaska-style competitions. In Scandinavia, skijoring without the pulk is predominantly viewed by many dog drivers as a training technique for Nordic-style mushing.

A Brief History

Scandinavians have used pulks—often pulled by reindeer—for hundreds of years to carry freight and necessities. The Scandinavian people historically have also been fond of animals, particularly the dogs that have been their faithful hunters, guards, and herders for so many centuries. The Norwegian elkhound, one of the oldest breeds of dogs still in existence, dates back to at least 4,000 BC. Dogs have accompanied the Scandinavian people at least since the Stone Age, twelve thousand years ago, and perhaps even longer than that.

When polar explorers and trappers brought the concept of Alaska-style dog mushing back to Scandinavia with them, it quickly became apparent that dog teams could be of immense help in trapline operations. But instead of adopting Alaska-style mushing, they invented a new form. Scandinavians are known for being "born on skis," so why not combine a dog team and a skier, which required fewer dogs than did Alaska-style mushing? Thus Nordic-style dog mushing was born.

Two historical events played an important part in increasing the popularity of both Nordic-style and Alaska-style dog mushing in Norway. One was Roald Amundsen's expedition with dogs to the South Pole in 1911. After Amundsen proved to the world how much you could depend on a dog team, many Norwegians became interested, built their own pulks, and used their house dogs to try out this exciting new sport. Mari has seen photographs of her father and grandfather hooking up their Norwegian elkhound and her father's goat. They would hitch up the animals tandem-style to pull their gear into their weekend cabin. Nordic-style mushing quickly found its niche in a country long accustomed to outdoor winter recreation.

A second strong influence on mushing's popularity came through several Scandinavians who traveled to Alaska as part of

One of the earliest Nordic-style sleds—called a Nansen sled—was named for Fridtjof Nansen (1861–1930), one of the arctic explorers who influenced Nordic-style mushing. The Nansen sled was a hybrid: its slatted basket was similar to dogsleds used by Alaska-style mushers, but it had a hand-operated brake and was designed for use by a skier.

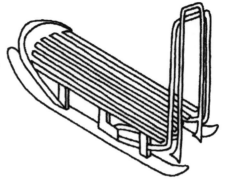

the gold rush. Most of them never saw much gold, but with their love of and understanding for animals, they soon caught on to Alaska-style mushing. Some took part in the first All-Alaska Sweepstakes in 1908, held in Nome. The winner of that race was a Norwegian, John Hegness. Another Norwegian, Leonhard Seppala (who later gained fame for his role in the historic Nome Serum Run of 1925), launched his illustrious competitive mushing career by winning this same race three years in a row.

In 1931, a handful of interested people in Oslo, Norway, founded the first Nordic-style mushing club, called Norsk Trekkhundklubb. Their goal was to place Nordic-style ambulance teams with drivers trained in first aid throughout the forests around Oslo. These teams would rescue injured skiers and bring them back to town. In this way, dog teams became accepted on the three hundred miles of ski trails that are maintained around the capital. In a short time the club earned respect and popularity from those who saw the benefits of these services.

Gradually, other clubs around the country were established, until in 1985 there were a total of fifty clubs in Norway. All these clubs belong to a common association called the Norwegian Dogmushers Association (Norsk Hundekjørerforbund), and they are also members of the Norwegian Sports Association.

Nordic-style races have been held in Norway since the 1930s. Until the 1980s, racing dogs were required to be purebred. The most common breeds used were the German shorthaired and wire-haired pointers, German shepherd, Greenland Eskimo dog, giant schnauzer, Irish setter, and Siberian husky. The short-haired dogs would run shorter distances of about eighteen miles; the "tougher" dogs (the thick-haired breeds) would run about thirty miles with a twenty-minute mandatory stop. In 1952 an exhibition Nordic-style race was held during the Winter Olympics in Oslo.

In 1959 Helge and Benedicte Ingstad imported the first Siberian husky to Norway. With these dogs, Alaska-style dog mushing was formally introduced to Norway. Since then, Alaska-style and

Nordic-style mushers have been working side by side, although not without a few conflicts of interest.

In the 1970s and 1980s, the biggest conflict arose over whether or not to restrict race participation to purebred dogs. Alaska-style mushers were interested in importing dogs from the United States that were not necessarily AKC-registered or even of pure breed. Many Nordic-style mushers wanted to bar unregistered breeds from racing. Eventually, all breeds became eligible to compete in Norway, registered or not. The dog drivers came to realize they needed to work together, instead of fighting, to preserve their trail systems and to maintain the sport's popularity with the public.

Equipment for Nordic-Style Mushing

The equipment required for Nordic-style mushing is more complicated and a bit more expensive than that required for skijoring. However, several options and configurations are available.

Pulks

Purchasing a pulk can be a significant expense; good pulks don't come cheap, nor should they. A well-made pulk is designed to be strong but flexible, is built to glide easily and handle well, and is constructed of high-quality, durable materials. A dog harness is a comparatively cheap and disposable item. If one doesn't work out, it can be easily replaced. A pulk, on the other hand, is an investment. If it's an investment you can't afford to make, you may want to fabricate your own, but it is unlikely you will be able to match the quality and durability of a commercial one.

Pulks come in several shapes and sizes and may be made of wood or fiberglass. They are built narrower than a dogsled to fit into ski tracks. Their low-to-the-ground nature allows for greater stability. The sides are usually about five inches high, although a full load can end up reaching much higher. An empty pulk normally weighs between eight and sixteen pounds. Two runners on the bottom of the pulk help to keep it stable and on track. The runners are sometimes made out of steel but more often are P-Tex or another type of hard fiberglass.

Commercial models range from small, streamlined competition pulks to roomy freight pulks. Child's pulks are designed for transporting young children, and a larger version is designed for adults. There is even a special rescue pulk. Pulks for children and people with disabilities come with windshields, safety harnesses, and plenty of padding. Competition and freight pulks normally include a cloth top and elastic cord system for lashing in loads.

Shafts

Before you decide to buy a pulk, consider how your dog will pull it. A pulk can be pulled two ways: by semirigid shafts or by a regular gangline such as those used in Alaska-style mushing. Shafts are most commonly made of aluminum or fiberglass. They attach to the pulk under the front rim, angle upward at a forty-five-degree angle, and then extend straight to the dog. Some shafts end in a bow that arcs over the dog's shoulders. This allows the skier to hold onto the shaft system when going downhill or when starting

ANDREA SWINGLEY

out. Hooks or snaps mounted on the sides of the shafts attach to the dog's harness, which is a slightly different style than a regular pulling harness. The dog needs room to stretch out, so the shafts should be roughly seven feet (about two meters) long. Shaft extensions allow the use of more than one dog.

Shafts have several functions. They keep the pulk from overrunning the dog, a big plus when going downhill or when the dog is first learning to pull. Shafts help the pulk track around corners and over uneven terrain, and they help to prevent tangles. Shafts do have some disadvantages, however. For example, the dog's harness must be specifically designed to clip into the shafts. Also, dogs

POLLY WALTER

The pulk on the right is set up to be pulled by a skier. The shafts are much longer than those of a pulk pulled by a dog. By changing the shafts, the pulk can be pulled by one or two dogs. Several pounds of gear can be carried in a pulk, and the average-sized dog can pull about fifty pounds.

The pulk in the middle, which is facing away from the viewer, is designed for use with three or more dogs and for carrying gear. A brake is attached on the back for safety. The front is equipped with a Nome hitch for running dogs with a gangline instead of shafts.

The pulk on the left is used for competition, with the shafts designed for use with a dog. A competition pulk is lighter and more streamlined than one used for recreation.

with unmatched gaits will not run as smoothly together in shafts, and a dog not trained to shafts may panic at their strange feel.

Pulks can also be pulled Alaska-style, with a gangline attached to the front of the pulk by means of a special pulk attachment called a "Nome hitch." This bar extension attaches to the front of the pulk to hold the gangline up and forward of the pulk's nose.

Brakes

When you use a pulk without shafts, you must be extremely careful to control the pulk so that it doesn't overrun the dog. You may want to purchase a brake, particularly for multidog teams or for hilly and uneven terrain. Ingeniously simple and easy for a skier to use, pulk brakes consist of two upright bars, each in the shape of an upside-

down U, attached to the back of the pulk. One bar is permanently fixed in the upright position; the other bar pulls downward by hand, driving its bottom points into the snow for braking.

Lines

The skier is attached to the pulk by means of a rope that runs from the front of the pulk, up through an antenna mounted on the back of the pulk, and from there to the skier's belt. The antenna elevates the rope to prevent it from tangling in your skis. The portion between the front of the pulk and the antenna is usually made out of bungee cord, while the last six feet or so between the pulk and the skier is usually regular poly rope.

Harnesses

If you use a gangline with the pulk, a regular Alaska-style dog harness works just fine. Shafts, however, require a different type of harness. The traditional Nordic-style harness consists of a thick leather collar and traces, similar to what you might see on a draft horse. When using shafts, the pulling force should come off the dog's neck, rather than off a tugline hitched to the back of the harness as in Alaska-style. Some harness makers have developed a modified webbing harness for pulk shafts that operates on the same principle as a leather harness. While much less expensive than leather, the modified webbing harness is not as effective for heavy loads.

The harness is actually the most important piece of equipment for Nordic-style mushing. The harness must fit correctly, because an ill-fitting harness can cause sores, affect pulling ability, and prevent the dog from using its full potential. A leather collar harness should lie snugly against the dog's neck *above* the shoulder bones, not on them. If the collar rests on the dog's shoulder bones, it will prevent the dog from moving freely and can cause sores.

Making Your Own Pulk

Making your own pulk may be an acceptable alternative to purchasing one, at least for short outings or experimental purposes. Many department stores carry plastic child's sleds (also known as "little red sleds") that, with a little modification, can serve as a low-budget alternative to a commercial pulk.

Keep in mind that although these lightweight sleds can prove remarkably durable, they are not designed for rough handling, huge loads, or major wear and tear. They should not be relied on for long touring trips. They are not appropriate for serious competition, although they're great for fun races. Because they're inexpensive, they make terrific "beater" sleds for short trips and light work.

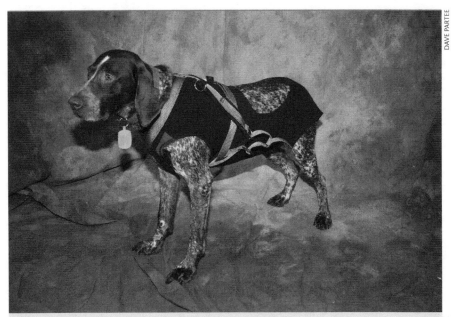

DAVE PARTEE

Loops on each side of this pulk harness are designed to attach to shafts.

However, you don't want to have to depend on one when you make your ascent of Mount McKinley or follow the Iditarod trail.

The sled will need to be modified slightly to work as a pulk. If you simply run a line directly from one or two holes in the front of the sled to the dog's tugline, you're likely to tear out the plastic as soon as you put a significant load in the sled. To create more durable rigging, weave a bridle of poly rope through holes in the back and along each side of the sled to the front, ending in a loop at the very front. This arrangement distributes the pulling force more evenly along the entire sled.

When packing the sled, distribute the load as evenly and as low as possible, placing the heaviest items on the bottom and toward the back. You may want to fabricate a sled bag to protect the load. Also, be sure to securely tie down your gear so that it doesn't shift around when you start up or go over uneven terrain.

Teaching Your Dog to Pull a Pulk

Using a pulk gives you the ability to go on overnight trips or to carry cargo into a cabin without using a big dog team. Or, if you burn with competitive fire, learning Nordic-style mushing may one day lead you to the international world championships. Regardless of your level of ambition, it's important to go step-by-step and to have the proper equipment.

Nordic-style mushing is more complicated for a dog to learn than skijoring. It also requires the dog to pull inert weight rather than an active skier. A dog's bone structure normally is not strong enough to pull a pulk until the dog is at least twelve months old. For these reasons, you should wait until the dog is a year old before introducing him to Nordic-style mushing, although you can introduce a younger dog to the shafts so that they will seem less foreign. You should know how to ski, and both you and your dog should know how to skijor. Find a quiet, soft, and snowy trail. A pulk is likely to be noisy on a hard trail, which may frighten the dog. Put a little weight in the pulk (just a few pounds) to reduce the amount of noise it makes on the trail, but make sure whatever you use for weight doesn't rattle or slide around.

Once you've prepared your equipment and you are ready to begin training, keep one thought uppermost in your mind. This first experience must be a positive one. Otherwise, your dog may not want to pull a pulk again. Remain absolutely calm and relaxed, project confidence, and be prepared to exercise plenty of patience when you introduce your dog to the pulk. Even a well-trained dog may become unnerved when asked to pull a foreign load while wearing a strange harness with rigid shafts on either side. That's a lot of unfamiliar stimuli to throw at a dog all at once. But almost any dog will come around with patience and a healthy dose of positive reinforcement.

For the first step, simply harness the dog and hook her into the shafts. Stand beside her (don't put on your skis just yet) and hold onto the shaft. If the dog appears worried or frightened, talk calmly and reassuringly to her. Then put a leash on her and begin walking her around, providing plenty of encouragement and praise. Give her a chance to become accustomed to the shafts and to the idea of something dragging behind her. (Training a younger dog to pull a drag such as a chain broom or small tire will have helped in this respect.)

Individual dogs will react differently to the first experience of pulling a pulk. One may lie down, another may try to bolt or twist to get rid of the pulk and shafts, and yet another may just stand there as if in shock. Keep working with your dog until she relaxes. It's extremely rare to find a dog that instantly takes to the experience. The difference between Nordic-style mushing and skijoring can be likened to driving a bus versus driving a car. Don't ask your dog to parallel park on the first run! As we said before, stay calm and be sure you are in a positive frame of mind. Set aside plenty of time to work with your dog. This kind of training shouldn't be done in a hurry.

Once you've gotten your dog over the initial hump of getting used to the shafts and pulk, the next step is to put on your skis and once again hold onto the side of the shaft. You should be attached to the pulk by a rope with a bungee, as described earlier. Make sure you have a proper skijoring belt with a releasable snap or open hook. Again, pick a flat, soft trail that the dog is familiar with and encourage her to pull while you hold onto the shaft. When you think the dog is confident enough, let go of the shaft and drop back so that she begins to pull from in front of you. Watch her carefully and reassure her if you see any signs of nervousness or fear.

If the dog remains confident, begin to ski behind the pulk. Don't become overambitious, however. Maintain a slow, easy pace and conclude the session after just a short distance. Remember, your goal is to make sure the dog loves this new activity and wants to do it again next time.

Before you head for hills or rough terrain, make sure your dog understands what you want him to do and is relaxed with the pulk behind him. If you are worried about falling when you go downhill, take the line off your belt and hold it in your hand. Go as slowly as you can, snowplowing to lower your speed, so that the dog feels as if he is pulling even when he is running downhill. Don't let go of the line if at all possible, because it can whip forward and strike the dog.

At the bottom of a downhill slope, the dog is pushed toward the ground by his own weight, the speed, and the pulk behind him. Don't stop snowplowing until your dog is *past* the bottom of the hill, and keep the line tight. Otherwise the dog may lose his balance.

Regardless of how easily your dog adjusts to the pulk, one to three miles at a time is enough to begin with. Gradually increase the mileage over time. To avoid burning out the dog, don't use the pulk too often. Those who train for Nordic-style competitions usually have their dog pull a pulk no more than once or twice a week, and they skijor the rest of the time. Also, what you put in the pulk for weight is important. Make sure the load doesn't make noise and won't shift around. Keep the weight at about forty pounds or less per dog.

If you don't have shafts on your pulk and are using a gangline, it helps to tie off the pulk or to have a second person hold your dog while you put your skis on. Use flat, soft, snowy trails that are wide enough for snowplowing so you can control the speed of the pulk. Always be careful that the pulk doesn't slide into the dog, because a dog can easily become fearful after just one bad experience.

Eventually, you may want to use more than one dog to pull the pulk. Remember that you must always be in control, and don't take out more dogs than you can easily handle. When you first go out with a multidog team, make sure the trail is in good condition—hard but not icy or noisy—to keep the dogs from being frightened or injured. A brake is helpful when you use two or more dogs. Also, try to combine dogs with the same running style. A trotter (a German shepherd, for example) and a loper (such as a German shorthaired pointer) will not work well together, particularly in shafts where the movements will run counter to each other.

In Alaska-style mushing, it's easiest to harness train pups in a team, with a competent leader in front of them. But in Nordic-style mushing, it's best to train each dog individually to pull the pulk. This teaches the dog to pull a weight, and the dog won't be overrun by a second dog. This is particularly important when using shafts. However, before you start training, it's not a bad idea to arrange for your dog to watch another dog pulling a pulk, if that's possible.

For those who enjoy winter camping with dogs but don't own a dog team, Nordic-style mushing is a great compromise. A well-trained dog can pull its own weight in gear, as long as the trail is not too steep or snowy. With a well-packed pulk, a well-conditioned dog, and the ability to ski, you can go just about anywhere a dog team can go.

ANDREA SWINGLEY

Your dog should be completely comfortable in front of a pulk before you add the high stress of competition.

10 Touring and Winter Camping

Skijoring and Nordic-style mushing give ski tourers a great advantage. If you love to ski into the backcountry, skijoring with a dog allows you to go farther, and Nordic-style mushing allows you to carry more gear. The dog's company is an added attraction in either case.

As in the chapter on learning how to ski, we don't intend to cover all the ins and outs of winter camping with dogs in this chapter. We'd simply like to share a few pointers we've learned. Please realize that winter camping and ski touring can be dangerous. Before you go out for the first time, and especially before you tackle difficult terrain or severe weather conditions, you should read up on the subject of winter camping in general and talk to experienced winter campers. Your first trips ideally should be undertaken with an experienced companion. Please don't depend on this chapter to tell you everything you need to know.

Plan Ahead

Winter camping with dogs requires forethought and planning. You should be well equipped and able to deal with both wet and cold conditions, and you should know how to take care of your dog. Both you and your dog should be healthy and in good condition, and you should have the proper equipment for skiing and camping.

Don't take a dog on a trip that you wouldn't be capable of doing without canine assistance. If you run into any trouble at all, you should be capable of getting out of it *without the dog.* If you can't do it alone, don't expect the dog to help you. In fact, for the first mile or so, it's likely the dog will make everything even harder and more complicated until he calms down. Also, remember that you are responsible for conserving your dog's resources. If you expect him to pull you into a cabin twenty miles down the trail, don't let him sprint out all his energy in the first five miles.

Choose a trip based on your level of experience and within both your and your dog's capabilities. During her very first winter camping trip, a friend of ours experienced an unfortunate mutiny: Her dogs quit and ran back to her truck, leaving her to pull her pulk back by herself. It's a wonder she ever wanted to go camping again. On the other hand, when Mari first went winter camping at sixteen years old, she accompanied some people who knew exactly what to do. Even at thirty below, Mari was never cold or uncomfortable. That first positive experience set the stage for many future adventures, including a trip with dogs partway up Denali (also known as Mount McKinley).

Being organized makes any trip at least twice as easy. If everything is neatly packaged, labeled, and well packed, you won't waste time trying to find a piece of equipment or figuring out which package holds tonight's dinner. It's miserable to have to search frantically through an untidy pile of gear when you're cold and wet. Know where each item is and have a certain place for everything. The extra time you spend preparing will pay off.

Make sure your sled or pulk is stable and not prone to tipping. This will depend partly on its design and partly on how you pack it. Put heavier items on the bottom, all waterproofed, and pack them

ROB LOVEMAN

as evenly as possible. Always pack an extra blanket to use in case of frostbite, hypothermia, or other emergencies.

Equipment for People

Tents

Whether you are going on an overnight or a two-week trip, you need basically the same equipment. If you use a tent, bring one that is designed for winter camping. Make sure your tent zippers work in the cold. Also, keep in mind that your tent will be filled with bulky winter gear. A four-person tent in the summer may be only a two-person tent in the winter.

When you pitch your tent, shovel out a spot below snow level and make a snow wall around the tent site to keep out the wind and to store your gear in. The snow wall will increase warmth and provide shelter for the dog. Be careful, however, not to tie your dog too close to the tent. Otherwise you may find yourself with an uprooted tent, unexpected air-conditioning, or unwelcome precipitation.

Sleeping Bags

Your sleeping bag should be rated for winter temperatures. In the Far North, where the weather tends to be colder but dry, a down bag works well. In damper climates, a synthetic bag that insulates when wet may be a better idea. A sleeping pad will increase your warmth as well as comfort. If you usually use an inflating pad, you might want to switch to a noninflating pad for winter camping, because the valves on inflating types tend to freeze up. Mari recommends a foam pad, which actually feels warmer to her than the inflating type. The snow is soft, so you shouldn't need the extra cushioning of an inflating pad. Mari has also used untanned reindeer hides and swears by them for keeping warm.

Camp Stoves

Most high-quality camping stoves work fine for winter camping. Make sure your stove works in the cold—and at high altitudes, especially if you will be traveling in the mountains. Test the stove before you leave and be sure you understand exactly how to run it. Also be sure to pack the right fuel for the stove you use.

Clothes

The more layers of clothing you wear, the more options you have for regulating your body temperature. You may start out skiing with as many as four layers of clothes that can be shed as you begin to warm up. It's important to avoid overheating. If you get too hot while working and begin to sweat, you'll become chilled when you stop.

The layer you wear next to your skin is important in cold temperatures. Long underwear top and bottom will increase your warmth. If you plan to ski hard, you'll probably want to wear a material that wicks moisture away from your skin. If you are an inactive skier, go for warmth over wicking. Keep in mind that even in mild weather you'll need to dress as if the temperature is lower than the thermometer reads. The wind you generate by skijoring cools you down considerably.

Breathable clothing is essential. Wool is a fine choice for long underwear if you can tolerate it next to your skin. Silk or polypropylene underwear works well while you are actively skiing, but may not be as warm a choice in camp. Avoid cotton, which dries slowly and won't keep you warm if it gets damp. Mari likes wool because it is so warm and insulates even when wet. If wool makes you itch, wear it as a second layer rather than right against your skin.

Head gear is important when you're skijoring because of the windchill. Be sure to wear a warm hat that covers the ears and has a wind-breaking shell. In extreme temperatures, consider a parka with a tunnel-type hood or a fur hat and face mask. You lose a great deal of body heat through your head, so a warm hat is essential. Using a monk's hood, also known as a balaclava, as the inner layer under a fur hat or hood can significantly increase its warmth. A scarf or neck gaiter will keep the wind out of the neck opening of your parka and can keep your chin and nose warm as well.

Good mittens or gloves are extremely important to the skijorer, just as they are to the regular cross-country skier. In colder weather, we find that a layering system works well. The bottom layer is a pair of thin gloves to give your fingers some protection when you have to do detail work with them. The next layer is a pair of warmer, well-insulated gloves, and for really cold weather, you might want to finish up with a pair of thick mitts. Realize that when your hands grip a ski pole, they can become quickly chilled because of restricted circulation. It's important to flex your fingers and palms periodically. Bring several changes of gloves and a warm pair of mittens for camp.

One of the most miserable conditions for a skier to endure is a pair of frozen feet. Wear warm socks (not cotton) that insulate when wet, and bring several extra pairs. Gaiters are helpful if you travel in deep snow. Ski-boot covers will keep your feet appreciably warmer in cold temperatures.

Wind pants are necessary in cold weather, and they can help you stay dry in warmer weather if you fall. Insulated coveralls under a thin, windproof anorak will keep you much warmer than will a thick parka with no extra covering over your legs.

Parkas and anoraks constitute your last layer. In cold weather, a heavily insulated parka may be necessary. In warmer weather, a light, windproof anorak may be the best choice.

Make sure you bring at least one dry change of clothes to use in camp. Three changes of clothing are ideal, but if you don't have the room for so much extra gear, you may have to wear sweaty clothes over again the next day. With three changes, you will also have a spare set if you fall through ice or otherwise get soaked. A cotton/wool blend of long underwear is a good choice for camp wear. A turtleneck, thick wool sweater, wool pants, and mukluks are also useful in camp (although mukluks should have waterproof covers). A heavy parka will keep away the chill of being less active.

When you get to your campsite, take your ski boots off right away but stay in your skiing clothes until you've finished tent digging and other sweaty tasks. As soon as you've set up your campsite, change into camp clothes. If you have room, you can hang your skiing clothes in your tent to dry. You also can dry them over your stove or campfire or, at the very least, keep them warm in your sleeping bag.

Be sure to put your boots in your sleeping bag at night. One winter, some Fairbanks skiers suffered severe frostbite when they camped overnight in cold temperatures. They left their boots outside their tents and in the morning put their feet into icy-cold footgear, reasoning that their body heat would warm up the boots. Not so. They ended up stranded at a cabin with badly frostbitten feet.

People Food

Bring food you like to eat! If more than one person is going on the trip, arrange to go shopping together so that you each can choose food you enjoy. To spark up your meals on the trail, prepare some hearty entrees ahead of time and take them along in freezer bags. Freeze-dried food may be convenient, but it gets boring after a couple of days. Always carry food for two or three extra days (this is when freeze-dried food comes in handy). Chili powder, Cajun spices, or curry powder can help liven up your meals and provide variations on the freeze-dried theme.

If you pack each meal in a waterproof bag and label each bag, you can simply pull out the appropriate bag for any given meal. For example, you might want oatmeal one morning and pancakes the next, so each can be packed separately in its own bag and marked for speedy retrieval. Supermarkets carry many easy-to-prepare meals that are great for camping. If you purchase a boxed meal such as macaroni and cheese, take the meal out of the box and make it into as small and light a package as you can, being sure to label the package. Include any cooking directions you'll need. This packaging method also works well for stashing food in a cache. Remember that some basics, such as pasta, cook up even more rapidly than boxed meals.

Remember to eat well and often. Being well fed will keep up your mood, increase your energy, and help to keep you warm. On a trip with two or three people, each can monitor how the others are doing. If one person stops eating, which may happen under stress or simply by oversight, it's important for the others to encourage that person to eat. Pack some high-powered snacks to eat along the trail. Nuts or trail mix are good choices, as is chocolate (of course!). If you have a favorite protein bar, pack it in an inner pocket of your skiing clothes so that it stays chewable.

Drink plenty of fluids when you're on a camping trip. Bring drinks you like, but take it easy on the caffeine. A cup of coffee at breakfast is fine, but remember that coffee acts as a diuretic. If you're fond of sports drinks, look for powdered or tablet forms that pack light and can be mixed with water on the trail. Plain water is most important: After breakfast, heat up some water and put it in a thermos or insulated water bottle so that you have hot water ready for lunch. A hot water bottle also can go in your sleeping bag at night to keep you warm—but make sure the container doesn't leak.

Equipment for the Dog

Figure the amount and type of dog equipment you need by how many dogs you are taking and how you plan to run them. If you are going to use a big pulk or a sled and three or four dogs, bring one or two extra harnesses in case one gets chewed up. It can be difficult to repair a harness on the trail. Bring booties. You won't know what conditions your dogs might be running in, and booties also can be used to protect sore or injured feet.

It's a wise idea to secure your dogs, especially at night. If you only have one or two dogs, they can either sleep in your tent or be anchored to nearby trees—if there are any!—or to your sled. Don't use your skijoring line or gangline as a picket rope unless you are sure your dogs won't chew it. (And don't forget to bring extra poly rope for emergency repairs.) If you bring a whole team, a cable picket or a cable-filled gangline can be used to tie out the dogs.

If you are running short-haired dogs, bring coats for

ROB LOVEMAN

A cable picket strung between trees keeps dogs safe and secure.

them. Even Alaskan huskies can be sparsely haired on their bellies or genitals; if your dogs need added protection, bring dog coats that are worn over the harness or belly blankets that can go right under the harness. The dogs appreciate the extra warmth, especially in the wind, and it will give them extra energy. Most sled dogs will chew off a blanket or coat if you leave it on them for any length of time, but if you put a coat over a dog that is tired, he's more likely to leave it alone. Get the dog used to wearing a coat before you go on the trip.

It's usually neither necessary nor feasible to haul straw for bedding. Spruce branches make good bedding for both you and your dog, but cutting spruce boughs may not be accepted practice in some areas. For one or two days at a time, snow is sufficient insulation if the dog has a decent undercoat. If you stay in one spot more than a few days, you may need to move the dogs around, as their beds of snow will turn icy. Some people bring blankets for the dogs

SIBERPOP PHOTOGRAPHY

A thick-coated dog, such as this Siberian husky, can tolerate even extreme cold with ease.

ROB LOVEMAN

Though they don't qualify as short-haired, these city-dwelling Siberians are happy to sleep in the tent. They are restrained by an internal dropline.

to sleep on, but most huskies or other sled dogs will eat blankets—an unfortunate habit that can leave you with a dead dog.

A short-haired dog with a sparse undercoat may be most comfortable in the tent with you, or at least in a sleeping bag of his own. Two or three dogs can pile into an old sleeping bag inside your tent, and they usually love it (provided they get along together). Short-haired dogs will generate more heat in a tent than a thick-furred dog. Even if a short-haired dog is able to tolerate the cold, keep in mind that it will sap the dog's energy.

Food for the Dog

Bring enough dog food for the planned trip plus a couple of extra days. Remember that the dogs use more energy on a long trip, so you need to increase the amount of fat and protein in their diet. Giving them an extra scoop of fat as a snack when you take breaks along the trail will make a big difference. Males sometimes will require more fat than females, but it depends on the individual dog's metabolism.

Bring food that the dogs are used to; don't change their diet just for the trip. If you usually feed a cheap brand of feed, don't suddenly switch to a top-of-the-line brand the day before you leave. Instead, increase fat and protein by adding supplements. A much better choice is to put the dogs on a high-quality diet for at least two weeks before the trip. Premeasure the portions and organize the meals for each day. Don't forget to bring snacks.

Water is extremely important for the dogs. Remember that a mere 3 percent dehydration leads to a 20 percent drop in performance. Plan a little extra time into your camping schedule to heat up water for the dogs. Some long-distance mushers have invented or modified stoves that heat water quickly. At night, if there's wood around, you may be able to conserve stove fuel by building a fire.

In the morning, the dogs should each have about a quart and a half of warm water and then shouldn't be run for about two hours afterward; watering them earlier in the morning will allow you to leave sooner. If you can't wait, water them a little less first thing and then water them again at lunch. You can either bait the water lightly to encourage the dogs to drink or make a thicker soup so that the dogs actually get a little meal for breakfast. A light, warm meal in the morning will make the dogs perform better and will keep their attitudes up. Please remember: *Dogs cannot get sufficient liquids by eating snow.*

Dinner should be a regular meal. You don't have to feed the dogs much more than usual, as long as the fat and protein content is increased. You don't actually have to cook the dogs' supper, as long as you mix in warm water to take the chill off. Be sure the dogs get plenty of fluid in the evening.

First Aid

Bring a first-aid kit for both people and dogs. Your veterinarian can recommend a list of first-aid items for your dog, or you can use the list at the end of the chapter as a guide. A trauma kit might include sutures, medicine for diarrhea, antibiotics, bandages, and painkillers. One time some friends of Mari's were on a hike in the mountains when two of their dogs got in a terrific fight. They had no sutures with them, so they stitched up one dog's gaping wound with yellow sewing thread. Incredibly, the stitches held and the wound did not become infected. But it would be much better to travel with the proper equipment.

You may want to bring a first-aid booklet to save time and energy. If someone goes into shock or becomes hypothermic, for example, you might not be able to remember the specific steps to take. If you have a book with you, you can look up the proper remedies in an instant. Even if you've been trained in first aid, a book can take off some of the pressure of remembering exactly what to do in the heat of an emergency.

A customized first-aid kit might include a list of contents, a checklist of what to do in various situations, and coins for a phone call in case you end up without cell phone coverage. Don't carry freezable medications. Use tablets rather than liquids whenever possible.

Some Safety Considerations

- Bring a map and compass with you and know how to read both before you leave. A GPS is a wonderful tool, but be sure you have a backup plan in case the battery fails. The same goes for a cell phone—it may be able to get you out of trouble as long as it works and there's coverage, but don't rely on it, especially in Alaska.
- It's best to travel with another person, but at the very least, make sure someone knows where you are going, what your

schedule is and when you should be expected back. Draw
your route on a map and leave it with someone reliable.
- Carry flares and wear bright clothing. A red or orange parka
makes you more visible.

- Become familiar with the characteristics of the area you'll be traveling in. Avoid avalanche country and be especially careful in weather conducive to avalanches: cold temperatures followed by warm and snowy weather. Avoid waterways that are known to be treacherous and watch out for overflow.
- When traveling across lakes or rivers, open your bindings so that you can remove your skis quickly if you fall through the ice. Take the ski-pole straps off your wrists and hold your poles loosely in your hands. Release your skijoring line from your belt and hold it in your hand.
- Carry an ice scraper in case you go through overflow, so you can scrape the ice and snow off your skis.

ROB LOVEMAN

Snowless approaches to a backcountry trail may require innovative solutions. The "land pulk" pictured here was created by mounting the pulk on a wheeled crawler used by auto mechanics.

Snow Caves

If you are stranded and need protection from the elements, or if you simply choose to use snow as your primary shelter, a snow cave is the best way to spend the night in snow. Snow caves are warm and windproof. When you excavate a snow cave, don't immediately dig straight down. Dig into the slope at a gentle downward angle, then steeply down toward the ground, then back up toward the surface. This makes a well at the entrance of the cave for the cold air to settle into and a higher sleeping platform at the back for warm air to be trapped in. For safety's sake, you may want to practice building a snow cave before you go on your trip.

Always poke a couple of holes in the snow cave roof for ventilation, and stick your ski poles through the holes to mark your location for others or in case you have to dig your way out. Don't forget to bring your shovel inside with you! Burn a candle all night to monitor the oxygen level, and don't completely close off the entrance. Use a backpack or other less-than-airtight block to shut out the cold air. Don't cook inside a snow cave too much, either, or the walls will begin to sweat.

Touring Checklists

These lists are not meant to be comprehensive. They are only meant as a starting point from which to develop your own list of necessary equipment. Plan carefully, whether for a day trip or five-week trek.

Clothes

First Layer (can be wool or polypropylene)
- Long underwear, top and bottom
- Inner socks or sock liners
- Hat or monk's hood that covers ears
- Scarf or neck gaiter
- Mittens or gloves

Intermediate Layer
•Knickers or skiing pants
•Shirt
•Sweater
•Outer socks
•Knee warmers

Outer Layer (should be bright colors—orange or red)
•Ski-boot covers
•Windproof anorak with hood and ruff
•Windproof mittens or overmitts
•Windproof pants
•Waterproof jacket/light rain gear (particularly in Lower Forty-eight or for long trips)

In Camp
•Turtleneck
•Heavy sweater
•Heavy jacket (down or synthetic)
•Wool or polar fleece pants
•Thick pair of snow pants
•Thick, warm socks
•Change of gloves or mittens

Tools
•Fid (for repairing lines)
•Pliers
•Screwdriver
•Knife
•Tape (duct tape works well)
•Wire
•Twine
•Cotton rope
•Screws

Ski Equipment
•Skis
•Bindings
•Boots
•Poles
•Wax
•Scraper (for overflow)
•Spare ski tip
•Spare pole basket (particularly important in deep snow)
•Spare binding parts

Food and Drink

- Warm drinks (tea, hot fruit drinks, bouillon, hot sports drinks)
- Oatmeal, pancake mix, or other nutritious breakfast
- High-fat soups for lunch
- Soups, casseroles, etc., for dinner (can bring favorite meal frozen into packets)
- Dried fruits, chocolate, nuts, protein bars for snacking and emergency (dried fruits should be soaked in water, or else they tend to create dehydration)

Camping Equipment

- Backpack (internal or external frame; external is sometimes better for heavy packs but can limit range of motion, making skiing more difficult)
- Labeled waterproof bags for spare clothes, first-aid kit, food, etc.
- Heavy-duty, unbreakable thermos
- Plastic bottle with insulated case (plastic bottle filled with hot water can go in sleeping bag to keep you warm)
- Wide-mouth thermos for carrying hot soups or casseroles
- Food (pack in labeled individual bags)
- Waterproof sunscreen (should be high SPF rating, particularly in mountains, and oil-based to help with dry skin)
- Zinc oxide or other extra protection for nose
- Sunscreen/moisturizer for lips
- Sunglasses
- Sleeping bag
- Sleeping pad
- Waterproof matches
- Cup and plate or bowl
- Cooking and eating utensils
- Cooking pans
- High-altitude, low-temperature cook stove
- Stove fuel
- Waterproofing for boots (such as mink oil)
- Map with waterproof case
- Compass
- Pencil
- GPS
- Cell phone
- Tent
- Shovel
- Candle
- Flashlight and/or headlamp
- Extra batteries
- Fire ribbon
- Flares

•Sewing kit
•Sewing awl
•Waxed thread or dental floss (waxed thread is best)

Dog Gear
•Extra snaps
•Picket
•Booties
•Extra poly rope
•Extra sections of gangline
•Extra tuglines
•Food bowls (bread pans are light and stack beautifully)
•Harnesses (including extras)
•Necklines (including extras)
•Ice hook (if using sled or to anchor picket)

First Aid (some items can be used for both people and dogs)

For People
•Thermometer
•Butterfly bandages and sterile strips
•Gauze pad and wrap
•Adhesive tape
•Moleskin for blisters
•Tongue blades (Popsicle sticks) for finger splints
•Sling
•Cotton sutures
•Antiseptic soap
•Antihistamine
•Aspirin
•Antibiotics
•Zinc oxide
•Personal medications (for allergies or other conditions)
•Antidiarrheal tablets
•Scissors
•Needle
•Survival space blanket

For Dogs
•Toenail trimmers (for split nails)
•Aspirin (buffered is best)
•Iodine solution (for washing wounds)
•Elastic wrap (such as Vetrap)
•Antibiotic ointment
•Oral antibiotics
•Eye antibiotic ointment

•Elastic tourniquet
•Cloth muzzle (for injured or panicked dog)
•Aluminum splint
•Foot ointment

ROB LOVEMAN

11

Skijoring With Children and People With Disabilities

Skijoring and Nordic-style dog mushing can easily become a family activity. With common sense and the proper equipment, even infants and toddlers can come along. Older children can skijor with a trusted family pet once they have learned to ski well and weigh enough to be able to control a dog. For children under six years of age, a child's pulk is recommended.

Pulks for Children

You can begin sharing your love of skijoring with your child when she is as young as nine months old, provided you have a safe and secure means of transporting her. You shouldn't bring a child younger than nine months, however, because until then the child doesn't have sufficient autonomic control over her body temperature.

The child's pulk should be made as safe as possible. Whether you are planning to purchase a pulk or to construct your own, there are some important safety features to look for. The pulk should be strong but also light and easy to tow. A plastic sled may seem like a cheap and easy way to take a child around the block, but it is neither strong enough nor safe enough to use on skijoring trails. A child's pulk should be stable and should have enough room for the child to either sit or lie down. To determine stability, look at the profile of the pulk and the rigidity of the shafts. Make sure the sides of the pulk slope outward from the bottom so that the pulk returns easily to a stable position after a swing. Rigid shafts also will increase stability.

A large protective screen of colored plastic should be standard equipment on any pulk designed to carry people. The screen will protect against strong sunlight, windchill, flying snow, branches, and ski poles. The screen will also absorb the shock if the pulk overturns.

A cotton apron around the opening where the child sits will prevent snow from falling down into the pulk and will protect the child from both wind and cold. The pulk should have a padded seat back, high enough to support the child's neck and resilient enough to yield to sudden tugs. The seat back should be able to lie flat if the pulk turns over. It helps to have an adjustable seat that

LYNN ORBISON

moves up and down, so the child can either sit or lie down and sleep. A safety strap is important so the child can't fall out. More recent child's pulks even have an optional roll bar in case the pulk tips over.

The layer under the child is actually more important than the layer on top. A thick piece of foam rubber or other insulated padding should be placed in the bottom of the pulk to provide both warmth and cushioning. In Norway, people often use sheepskin sleeping pads that are both warm and comfortable, but any kind of sleeping bag or thick blanket can be used.

The child should be dressed in warm, loosely fitting winter clothing that allows him to move around comfortably and doesn't restrict his circulation. He should wear outer garments in which he can walk around if he gets restless in the pulk. Remember that the child is sitting still and will not be generating heat through physical activity. Extra garments will be needed in comparison to what the child would wear during normal play. If the child is too young to walk around, try putting mukluks or thick socks on his feet rather than winter boots. The child also should wear a warm, wind-resistant hat that covers the ears.

In colder weather, a sleeping bag, warm blanket, or thick rug should be used in the pulk in addition to the padding on the bottom. Bring extra gear for the child. Make sure that the child's hands are inside the bag and only the face is exposed. On the other hand, monitor the child's temperature so that he doesn't overheat! Keep in mind that strong sunlight may heat up the pulk until it becomes too warm for the passenger. You should be able to determine how the child is faring by slipping your hand inside the pulk to gauge the inside temperature. The child may need sunglasses if the sun is out, although the windshield is fairly protective.

If you don't have an absolutely trustworthy and well-trained dog, we don't recommend having a dog pull your child in the pulk. It is safer to pull the pulk yourself, using longer shafts and wearing a belt with side rings designed to hook to the shafts.

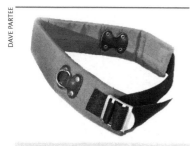

The rings on each side of this belt are designed to clip into pulk shafts.

When the child is older, or if your dog can be trusted, you can ski behind the pulk. A safer method is to hook the pulk behind you and the dog in front of you so that you are in the middle of the team. Need we mention that a releasable line from you to the dog is essential? You'll also need to be a competent skier if you are going to have a dog pull both you and a pulk behind you, especially on a tricky trail.

Keep your trips short and check the child at regular intervals to make sure he is comfortable. Generally, children easily become accustomed to riding in the pulk. When Mari's son, Gard, was very young, he tended to fall asleep in the pulk. During winter days when the temperatures were moderate, he would take his naps outside in the pulk while Mari worked in the yard.

To be safe, take your young child out only when temperatures are above zero, and don't forget to factor in windchill. If it is windy and cold, or if the temperature is low and will probably not rise

The safest way to transport a small child is to pull the pulk yourself. The child's pulk shown has a tinted windshield, a well-padded seat, and an adjustable backrest for the child's comfort.

much during the day, it is better to keep younger children at home. Keep in mind that a very young child cannot tell you how hot or cold he is; constant monitoring of the temperature inside the pulk may be your only way of determining the comfort of the child.

When planning a trip with a child, it is better to stick with familiar terrain. Safety should always be the primary consideration.

Teaching Children How to Skijor

Children can start skiing as soon as they can stand up on skis, but you have to keep the sessions short and the activity fun. When your child is between two and four years of age, she'll probably want to imitate you if she sees you skiing. Poles aren't necessary for the first couple of years that the child is skiing; the child learns better balance without them. It might not be a bad idea, if your child is interested, to send her to a skiing school. It's sometimes easier to learn an activity from someone other than a parent.

A young child on skis can hold onto a rope behind you as you skijor, as long as she is proficient enough on skis and enjoys the activity (and you have a trustworthy dog pulling you, of course). The age at which a child is ready to start skijoring alone will depend greatly on the individual, but certainly not before six years old, and only with a well-behaved and well-trained

MAGALI PHILIP

This child learned to ski when he was not quite two years old. (He is nearly three years old in this photo.) He customarily skis without poles.

223

dog. The child needs to know how to control the animal and should be an experienced skier. Don't hook the child up with a belt. Instead, have him hold the line so he can let go instantly. Choose a flat, easy trail, and make sure the child is ready for the activity. A negative first experience can undermine his future enthusiasm for the sport.

When a child first learns to skijor, an easygoing, mellow dog should pull her. Wider touring skis and boots with higher ankles provide added stability for the young skijorer. Shorter skis give more control. Start the child on familiar terrain within eyesight of the parent, or ski next to the dog until the child is comfortable with the experience of being pulled. Be sure that the trail is safe, well blocked off, and far away from any major problem areas such as roads or drop-offs. Keep the experience easy and enjoyable.

Mari believes a child shouldn't have his own dog to train until he is mature enough to be involved in all aspects of ownership, because younger children don't fully comprehend all the responsibilities. If a child is given a pup, it will take at least a year of training before the child can skijor with that pup. But the learning that takes place when a child brings up a pup, rather than being handed a dog that already knows how to pull, is markedly greater.

At age fourteen, Mari had to buy her own first dog, and it both demonstrated and cemented her level of commitment. A child who has a dog team handed to him with no requirement of commitment on his part may never develop the same degree of love and sense of responsibility for the sport. Sometimes, familiarity breeds contempt. A child who grows up with dogs and who sees dog driving as mundane may end up pursuing other interests. If a child doesn't show interest, we don't believe in pushing that child. The child often gets burned out from being pressured into something that isn't really in his heart.

If a child is truly interested in skijoring, he should have a few responsibilities to go along with the pleasure of the activity itself. How those responsibilities are presented, however, will make a big difference in how the child perceives them. Carol saw this principle in action one spring when her ten-year-old friend Sarah visited Carol's kennel for a dogsled ride. Sarah had been interested in dog mushing for a long time, but it wasn't feasible for her to have a dog of her own. She was fascinated by Carol's dogs and visited each one before the ride began. She loved riding in the sled, showed no fear at all, and stood on the runners with Carol on the way home.

In response to Sarah's enthusiasm and natural abilities, Carol hooked up her most trustworthy dog and sent Sarah off with her very own one-dog team. Sarah took immense delight in giving rides to her two younger brothers and handled the sled like a pro. But what surprised Carol most was Sarah's intense desire to help in the dog yard. When it came time to water the dogs after the rides were over, Sarah pleaded for the chance to carry the water bucket and ladle out the water. She welcomed this chore as an opportunity to do one more thing with the dogs.

If you make dog care a heavy responsibility for a child, it may become something he *has* to do, something unpleasant and necessary that has been handed to him. For Sarah, working in the dog yard was a treat and an opportunity, something she herself asked for and took great delight in.

Skijoring With People With Disabilities

Skijoring with people with disabilities can be an exceptionally rewarding experience. It's important for both the physically and mentally disabled to be given the opportunity to go outdoors and see the woods and the mountains. Snowmachines can serve the same purpose as dog mushing and skijoring, but the advantage of a dog team is that it is quieter than a snowmachine and incorporates the powerful therapeutic force of animals.

Skijoring with people with disabilities is similar to skijoring with a child: You should use trustworthy dogs that are accustomed to people and don't spook at strangers or noisy situations. Be sure the pulk you use is comfortable to ride in, with a thick bottom pad and a sleeping bag or other warm covering. The passenger should be dressed warmly and in windproof clothing. His comfort should be monitored closely throughout the ride. If the pulk doesn't have a windshield, sunglasses or goggles are a must. Some pulks are specifically designed for transporting people with disabilities, with a windshield, a special seat, and a brake on the back for greater control.

Choose a well-maintained trail system with terrain the dogs can handle while pulling an adult. If your passenger is timid,

Dryland work with people with disabilities can include wheelchair mushing. This dog's harness includes a handle so the dog can pull beside the wheelchair as well as in front of it. For rougher trails, a third wheel attached to the front of the wheelchair lifts the casters off the ground. This converts the wheelchair to a sort of tricycle with two large rear wheels and one medium front wheel.

choose flat, quiet, easy trails that won't be frightening. Some become bolder with time and eventually take delight in a more exciting ride. Keep the speed down and the distance fairly short. It's important to know what your passenger can handle and what you can expect of your dogs. It's also a good idea to bring along a handler who will ski or skijor with you and help out where needed.

Be well prepared. Remember to bring first aid with you when transporting children and people with disabilities. It might be a good idea to bring snacks and something to drink. You might consider taking along a picnic and stopping for lunch on the trail.

If you would like to set up a program for taking out people with disabilities, your first step might be to talk to a staff member of an organization for people with disabilities and, if possible, take that person out skijoring. If the person shows interest, she may even want to accompany you as a handler. Another way to garner interest might be to set up a passenger race, with trophies for the participants.

Norway has a large health and sports center with a special education program. Participants spend a month or two receiving therapy for disabilities such as accident-related injuries or blindness. The center is heavily oriented toward sports in its efforts to retrain the body, and it keeps dogs in residence for use in recreational, therapeutic activities. Some participants learn to drive their own dog teams as part of the program. Using sled dogs in work with people with disabilities is an area of therapy that we would like to see expanded in the United States, following Norway's excellent example.

12 Competition

Some people become involved in a sport with competition as their ultimate goal. Others fall into racing more serendipitously but become hooked once they get started. For some, winning is everything. "Recreational racers" simply compete for fun. They are unlikely to bring home any trophies, but they come across the finish line with smiles on their faces.

Why race? There are lots of good reasons and some that are not so good. Racing to win is a fine reason, as long as you don't lose sight of the welfare of your dogs. Burning with competitive fire doesn't give you the right to toast your dogs.

Racing is exciting. Competition can generate contact with new people, new places, and new ideas. Whether you are serious or just out to have fun, competing can provide direction and purpose to your training program. You and your dogs may benefit from a set schedule and a goal. Racing can also improve overall dog care. A competitive dog needs the best in everything: warm housing, top-quality feed, excellent veterinary care, and lots of time and attention.

The purpose of this chapter is twofold: to present some ideas and training tips for the beginning competitor, and to highlight the importance of the dog's welfare during both training and racing.

For the recreational racer, the ideas in this chapter can be used as a guideline for maintaining healthy, well-conditioned dogs and for doing acceptably well in a race.

For the serious competitor, these ideas are only a starting point. We've left out such topics as racing strategies, fine-tuning your equipment, detailed physical conditioning for both human and canine, and psychological tactics. Competitive dog driving is a book-length subject in itself. We suggest you read several other books on competitive dog mushing (see the Bibliography) and competitive cross-country skiing.

A Little Background on Races

Alaska-style dog-mushing races have been around for more than one hundred years in the United States. Likewise, Nordic-style

When competing, know your dog's capabilities. This experienced racer and dog negotiate a downhill turn at top speed.

competitions have been held for about eighty years in Europe. Most races of either type fall into two categories: sprint races (also called "speed races") of three to thirty miles and mid- and long-distance races of 150 to 1,000 miles. In Europe, the longest distance race is the Finnmarksløpet, with two sled classes: a 500-kilometer (310.7-mile) eight-dog class and a 1,000-kilometer (621-mile) fourteen-dog class. Most people in North America are familiar with long-distance racing because of the Iditarod Sled Dog Race from Anchorage to Nome, but there are actually many more sprint races than distance races. Sprint races tend to receive less publicity, however, and so are less well known.

Nordic-style races in North America are uncommon, and many skijorers are unfamiliar with the sport. In Nordic-style races, weight is added to each pulk in a set amount (forty pounds, for example) per dog. The addition of weight enables a one-dog team carrying forty pounds to compete directly with a two-dog team carrying eighty pounds or a three-dog team carrying 120 pounds.

Although both Nordic-style mushing and skijoring races involve a skier driving a dog in harness, the addition of a pulk changes some of the dynamics. The dog pulls the inert weight of the pulk, rather than the active weight of the skier. The skier in a Nordic-style team is therefore less able to affect the workload of the dog than the skijorer, who is directly attached to the dog. The Nordic-style skier is also less affected by the dog's actions, and the skier's own athletic abilities play a more important role.

One big difference between Nordic-style mushing and skijoring becomes immediately apparent in distance racing events: The pulk is used to carry camping gear and supplies, eliminating the need for the skier to carry a heavy backpack. Another difference is the lack of a direct physical link between the skier and the dog in Nordic-style mushing. The complicating element of the pulk and shafts also comes into play. Skijoring—and its dryland counterpart, canicross—is the simplest and most intimate form of dog driving there is.

Dryland racing has been rising in popularity: the 2011 International Federation of Sleddog Sports (IFSS) World Championship Dryland, held in Borken, Germany, in November, attracted twenty-three countries and 418 participants. Dryland competitions are usually divided by type (canicross, bikejoring, gig, etc.), and within each type are divided further by number of dogs and often by men's and women's classes. In the gig classes, dogs must be at least twelve months of age, and bikejoring dogs must be at least eighteen months old. Men and women compete together in the gig divisions but are in separate classes in bikejoring and canicross.

Distances for the dryland competitions tend to be shorter than those of winter races, and teams are not yet racing at top speeds. This works well for serious competitors, who can race early in their training regime by competing in dryland in the fall and then shift their focus toward racing for longer distances on snow in the winter.

What to Expect in Skijoring and Nordic-Style Races

Nordic-style races are separated into men's and women's classes, and usually have two subclasses, one-dog and multidog. With three or more dogs, a brake is required. A one-dog pulk has to be a minimum of 110 centimeters (about three and a half feet); pulks used in multidog classes must be at least 120 centimeters (close to four feet).

The stronger a skier you are, the more you can assist the dog (although the skier is not allowed to actually help the dog pull the pulk). To be truly competitive, you need to be a top-notch skier and you need a fast, strong dog, usually about fifty to seventy pounds. Dogs used for Nordic-style mushing tend to be bigger than skijoring dogs because they are pulling more weight. German short-haired pointers are extremely popular in Europe because of their size and speed.

Skijoring races are often divided into one-dog, two-dog, and sometimes three-dog classes. North American races aren't normally divided into women's and men's classes. (Particularly in the one-dog class, this may create the same inequity that prompted the separation of men's and women's classes for Nordic-style races. Given dogs of equal ability, male skijorers hold a distinct advantage over female skijorers.)

In recent years, mass starts for skijoring races—where all competitors line up together and start at the same time, typically in a wide area that eventually narrows down to a race trail—have become more popular. Mass starts require dogs that are well behaved in harness, are nonaggressive, and have a high tolerance for the proximity of other teams. It's also important for the skier to be able to skate without using poles at the start, as flailing poles create an extreme hazard for other teams.

Tips for Competition
Attitude

When you first start training for competition, you and your dog will both benefit if you realize that winning takes time and experience. It doesn't usually happen overnight. Be patient. Set your sights as high as you wish, but begin with the understanding that you are learning (and the best racers learn something new every time they compete). Enter the world of competition step-by-step, and you will be more likely to move up and stay up than if you are blinded by premature visions of a first-place finish. Don't let that glittering trophy block your view.

Contact and Control

If you want to become a competent racer, you must have control over both your dog and yourself. If you don't have close, day-to-day contact and communication with your canine partner, it doesn't matter how many hours you train or how much money

DAVE PARTEE

Having fast dogs naturally driven to run is just one component of consistent, top placing in races. Commitment, good training, and a positive attitude are all vitally important.

you spend on the latest equipment. Likewise, you need to exercise self-control. Common sense, a tight rein on your temper, and the ability to keep a level head under fire are all attributes you'll need at some point in a competitive career.

Your Dog's Diet

When a dog is under stress from sustained exertion, high-quality, complete nutrition becomes vital. A racing dog often runs much longer and harder than a recreational dog and is under much more stress. Your house dog may be able to subsist on average-grade dog food, but a racing dog cannot perform well without a high-quality diet.

Ideally, your dog should be on a high-quality diet year-round. At the least, this diet should begin *no later than when your training starts.* It may take two to six months before the benefits of a better diet are fully realized. (Likewise, you yourself should be eating a high-quality diet year-round, or at least from the beginning of training. You can't compete any more effectively by subsisting on potato chips than your dog can by eating cheap dog food.) Many competitive dog drivers choose diets consisting of premium (high-protein, high-fat) commercial feed mixed with various amounts of meat and other supplements.

Don't change your dog's diet in the middle of the racing season just because your competitor is feeding something that seems to work better. Change diets only if you have a strong reason to believe your existing diet is inadequate. If your dog is too skinny, don't add a lot of extra fat just before a race, and if your dog is too fat, don't put him on a radical diet just before you compete. You can't fix a nutritional error overnight. Many experts say it takes as long as three months for a dog's physiology to adjust to a new diet.

Training the Competitive Skijoring Dog

(For a detailed training regime, refer to Mari's suggested training calendar later in this chapter.)

The four qualities you want to enhance when you train a competitive skijoring dog are endurance, speed, strength, and responsiveness. A dog has to have all four for you to be a serious competitor.

No dog can run at top speed for twelve miles. But a racing dog develops a basic speed or pace and, if well conditioned, will maintain that pace whether in a four-mile run or a twelve-mile run. When you hear someone say a particular driver has her team on "cruise control," it refers to this basic speed.

To build and keep this basic speed, increase training mileages gradually and be sure the dogs are ready before you move them up from, say, three miles to five miles. The dogs should be finishing the day's run happy; they shouldn't immediately lie down and appear tired. They should be coming home strong. It's important to develop this solid foundation. A dog can't maintain his basic speed if you move his mileage up too fast, before his body is ready.

If the dogs tire at first when you increase mileage, stop and rest them close to home, then whistle them up and encourage them to finish hard. We don't recommend stopping too often, though. If you stop too much, the dogs begin to feel that they *should* stop. If you keep going, they learn to take breaks by easing up in harness as they run. Often, during a longer run, you'll see a dog slack off just a little bit and then recover. This is normal. (One way to sour an honest dog is to harp at him for taking a needed break.)

If your trails don't give you many choices for intermediate miles, and you have to bump your dogs up from, say, seven miles to twelve miles, they will come home fairly slowly during that first week of twelve miles. Introduce extra stops to encourage them to maintain their pace while they're building endurance. Gradually they will build up both their endurance and their lung capacity. Speed will follow. In the beginning, if you see that the dogs are getting tired, don't push them. Never pressure a dog to do something before he is physically ready for it. If you put pressure on too early, your dogs may learn to dive off the trail, dip snow (grab mouthfuls of snow while running), or develop other bad habits.

Remember that the main principle in training longer miles is to build endurance and to develop a team that is athletically fit all season. If your goal is to run in the championship races in March, don't cut back on your mileage in December just because preliminary races are shorter. Instead, try to strike a balance between enough miles to keep your dogs in condition and enough control over their speed to pick up the pace in short races.

Your goal is to maintain the dog's mental and physical health throughout the entire season. If you work your dogs too hard, too soon, they are going to burn out long before the championships—which are what count if you are going to be a serious competitor.

Summer Training

Whether training for sprint or long distance, you always start by building the same base. Summers are a relaxing time of year for the dog and should be devoid of any pressure. One or two long, leisurely runs per week are plenty. If you can't run your dog loose, take her out on a leash. Keep summer training fun and use the time to get to know your dog better.

An excellent way to exercise your dog is to take her swimming. If you have access to a lake and your dog likes to swim, you can either swim or canoe beside her. If you use a canoe, be sure to keep the dog ahead of or beside you. Don't lose sight of the dog behind you, and don't tie her to the canoe. Obviously, make sure the dog does not become tired and don't go too far from shore.

Bike training works well as summer exercise, but avoid hot sun and temperatures over sixty-five degrees Fahrenheit when you go out. Keep the training runs short. Because the dog shouldn't be subjected to heavy training in the summertime, some people don't even start bike training until the fall. Try to avoid asphalt roads; use gravel roads or trails in the woods. If you have to bike on asphalt, consider using booties but be prepared for them to wear out rapidly. Be extra careful and check your dog's pads often for abrasions or heat blisters. Hot asphalt can severely burn a dog's pads. If it's too hot for you to walk barefooted on the asphalt, don't ask your dog to do it either.

Your priority in the summer is to maintain muscle tone and to keep your dog motivated and happy. It's a time to wind down and relax, so that you and your dog retain a positive mental attitude.

Fall Training

When the weather starts to cool off, bike training can be done a couple of times a week. If you want to get really fancy, a four-wheeler or cart allows you to train more dogs at once. Running and walking on foot is excellent conditioning for both of you. Use your judgment in choosing how far to go, based on what kind of shape you and your dog are in. One lesson to teach your dog in the fall is how to run up hills. Take the dog out in harness, wear your belt and skijoring line, and do strength training (for both of you!) by running up steep hills.

You can train as often as four or five times a week, but don't worry about speed at this point and be careful not to overdo it. In the fall, the primary focus is on building a good base of endurance and strength. You shouldn't put much emphasis on speed just yet. Your goal right now is to teach the dogs to pull honestly and consistently.

Winter Training

In Alaska, the winter season can be divided into four parts. The first part, in November and December, is a transitional period when the terrain changes from dirt to snow. In December and January, preliminary races and a few bigger races may be held. The racing season peaks in February and March, when the biggest races are held. In April, the postrace season, you may find a few final races in the mountains.

When the snow falls, begin training on skis as much as possible. Whether you are training for skijoring races or pulk races, most of the time you should skijor. Skijoring is a low-stress way for the dog to learn to run fast without being afraid of speed, but don't run the dog as if you're racing all the time. Running a dog too fast can be scary for him, particularly if he is running next to a faster dog that is pushing him to go faster than he's ready for. When training, it's better to take out no more than two dogs at a time. Skijoring with one dog at a time gives you more training as a skier and lets you concentrate on the individual dog. You also have greater control, which is a vital element of all your training programs. Skijoring with two dogs seems to boost the dogs' morale and can be an effective way to add extra enthusiasm to your team.

As we've advised before, when you skijor down hills, snowplow to give the dog the feeling he is still pulling and to keep him from being frightened by the speed or by the possibility of being run over. The dog should be able to trust the harness and feel confident about leaning into it even when running downhill.

Using different trails for different types of training makes it easier for the dog to adjust to the training program. You can't verbally explain to your dogs, "Today we're going to take it easy and slow, and tomorrow we're going to do interval training," but if you use different trails for each type, they will begin to understand. Also, don't train too often on the same trail you'll be racing on, if you can avoid it. The race trail should be exciting for the dogs, and the training trail should be where you do your discipline training and conditioning.

Discipline training is the process of asking for and enforcing obedience. It is important that your dog does what you want him to do whenever you ask something of him. However, you should never stop and correct a dog during a race unless it's for aggression. It is bad for your team's attitude and will negatively affect any other teams that may be present. Discipline problems should be worked out early in the season, before you hit the race trails.

Don't act as if you are racing every time you go out on a training run, and don't nag your dogs unnecessarily during training. Some skijorers are naturally chatty, and their dogs learn to ignore all but the clear-cut commands, but constant encouragement or griping at a dog is counterproductive. Focus on good behavior and hard work, but don't put a lot of pressure on the dogs. The dogs will quickly learn the difference between training and racing.

Early Training for Nordic-Style Races

If you plan on competing in Nordic-style races, you should ski-jor for at least three to four weeks before you begin using the pulk. When you begin training with the pulk, remember that too much of it can sour a dog. There's a fine line between adequate pulk training and overdoing it. Use it just once or twice a week until mid-January. This will be sufficient for you and your dog to develop the necessary strength and for the dog to learn what it's all about. Start out with short miles, perhaps three miles or so, even if you've been skijoring longer distances. Gradually work up to ten miles—or whatever mileage is appropriate for the distance you plan to race.

Begin your pulk training by carrying half the weight you will race with. For example, if forty pounds is race weight, start with twenty pounds. Then gradually increase the load until you're at full weight by about the middle of January. By then the dog should be accustomed to both the weight and the distance. Start on fairly easy terrain when you train with the pulk. Save hilly trails for later. Your goal is to teach the dog how to pull a pulk and enjoy it at the same time. Don't overdo the distance; otherwise, both speed and motivation will go down. You may also injure the dog. Most injuries occur in dogs that are not adequately conditioned or are overly tired.

If your dog needs to build extra strength and you feel she is ready for it, gradually add extra weight to the pulk (working up to about ten pounds more than race weight) and do this strength training once a week until the middle of January. With the extra weight in the pulk, drive for five to seven minutes on short hills. Stop and rest, then do it again for five to seven minutes. This is similar to interval training for speed. The rest stops should be adequate to give the dog a breather. If possible, let the dog run loose for a few minutes. It's more difficult for the dog to just stand still for five minutes.

To add variety to your Nordic-style training regime, have your dog pull a pulk while a friend skijors ahead with another dog. This teases the pulk-pulling dog toward more speed and power, since she will have to work harder to keep up with the skijoring team. You can also train with a dogsled. Dogs don't seem to become as sour pulling a sled—perhaps because the load isn't as heavy—but it is still more work than skijoring, so it builds strength. Everything has to be kept fun, particularly for bird dogs and hounds that compete in

Nordic-style races. Alaskan huskies and other northern breeds seem to have a stronger instinct to pull even if it's not fun.

If you have several dogs and don't have time to take each one out individually, sled training allows you to train multiple dogs at one time. Running six dogs in front of a light sprint sled will give you about the same training effect as skijoring with two dogs. For early sled training, use a toboggan or heavier basket sled. You'll have more control and the dogs will learn to pull well.

Don't let the dogs run too fast at first, because they can be injured if they are not physically and mentally prepared for high speeds. The dogs are not ready to run at top speed with the first snowfall. You are only starting to build toward that point. Prevent the dogs from running flat out down hills, and keep your team small so that speed and power are under complete control. If a dog holds back, seems tense or worried while running, or looks back over her shoulder several times during a run, you may be going too fast for that dog.

A slower training sled also helps in fall leader training. When you try out a dog in lead, you don't want to go too fast because the speed may frighten the dog. If you acquire a new dog, running her in a team (not in lead) in front of a dogsled can help her adjust to your other dogs and can give you the opportunity to evaluate her abilities.

Skiing with your dog loose once a week will help keep up his motivation and attitude. This step seems especially important with hounds. When a dog is loose, you also can observe his natural gait and can see whether he's hurt or stiff. This will give you a basis for making judgments about a dog's readiness for the next step in training. (Skiing with a loose dog should be done only in unpopulated areas. Please don't ski with loose dogs on dog-mushing trails.)

Racing Season

As the racing season approaches, increase your mileage and frequency of training. Even if the skijoring or pulk races you'll be competing in are short distances (three to five miles), it's best to train longer miles to build the dog's endurance. In Norway, the *shortest* race is seven miles, and some races are eighteen to twenty miles long with only one dog pulling a pulk.

Mari doesn't advise training a dog for less than eight miles once you have built up to that distance. It's difficult to get a dog into condition if you always run short miles. Kathy Frost, who competed in every class of sled dog races from three-dog to open, said that even if you train more times a week, you simply can't build up the best muscle tone by running short miles.

When you run shorter miles, your dog never has a chance to settle down. A longer run reduces the stress and gives the dog a chance to relax in harness. It also gives you time to teach good manners and to do some real training, instead of just hanging on for a few exciting miles. The dogs are happier with that kind of schedule than with one where you're always racing at top speed.

During midwinter training, you can hold an interval training session once a week, while the other days should be longer, easier runs. Interval training, which is used to build speed, involves running at high speed for short distances. For example, sprint your dog for four or five minutes, then walk or run easily for five minutes, and then do it again. Do this about six times and then call it a day.

When you begin competing in the early races, you should still keep to your training schedule, and you may want to increase your miles even more. As the season progresses, you can begin to cut back on training and start to implement your racing strategy.

By February, the dogs should have developed enough speed, strength, and endurance so that you can focus on maintaining their condition instead of building it. You'll need to maintain that condition during the peak racing season, which in Alaska means through March. This can be tricky. At this point in your training, resting the dogs is just as important as running them. Many people overtrain at this point and end up with sour or injured dogs.

Once you've begun racing, don't use your pulk in training. Between pulk races, either skijor or use a dogsled. (If pulk races are few and far between, you can continue to train with the pulk once a week.) Concentrate on speed, motivation, and health. If you keep the dogs on top—happy and healthy—and avoid stressing them during training, you will have a winning team.

Resting for Races

It's customary to give the dogs two days off before a two-day race and one day off before a one-day race. For a race that runs Saturday and Sunday, train the dogs Tuesday and Wednesday and lay them off Thursday and Friday. Some people make the mistake of running their dogs the day before a race because they don't think the dogs have run enough miles. The dogs end up so tired by the time they actually race that they can't perform well. On the other hand, sometimes laying the dogs off for two days won't work with your schedule, and Mari's teams have done very well with one less day off. Evaluate your team—do your dogs seem tired and overtrained, or are they overeager? Mari finds that a long, slow, relaxing run on a Thursday before a sprint race is not always a bad idea.

The training you do on Tuesday and Wednesday before a weekend race should be easy for the dogs. Go the mileage you think they need; if you are racing a ten-mile race that weekend, you might run the dogs eight to ten miles each training day of that week. Some of this will depend on the weather: If it's cold (minus twenty-five degrees Fahrenheit or lower), sometimes it's better to sacrifice a little conditioning for the sake of avoiding cold-related injuries such as sliced pads and frostbite. Traveling may fatigue the dogs, so if you have to travel to the race, the dogs will need extra rest.

You may want to lay the dogs off for three days before a three-day championship. They should be in such good shape by now that they don't need conditioning. If you can let them loose, they'll get just enough exercise to stretch out and feel better. You may need to take them on a short run to see who is healthy and who is sore, in order to decide whom to use in the race. Sometimes a short run will speed the dogs up before a race, but be sure not to run short on the trails you'll be racing on, or the dogs will try for that shortcut during the race.

When you evaluate your team to decide which dogs to race, keep in mind that a well-conditioned dog that is familiar with racing may not do as well in training but will perform much better when it comes to the actual race. For the most part, you simply need to make sure that the dog moves freely, has sound feet, and is in good general health. If one dog seems marginal, take a different dog. There's a saying that drivers win races by the dogs they leave at home.

Race-Day Logistics

Feeding

To get the best performance out of your dogs, feed them approximately eighteen to twenty-two hours before the race starts. If your race starts at noon on Saturday, feed the dogs Friday afternoon about three p.m., even if you usually feed at five p.m. Some people decrease the amount of food and add more water, but that may not be as effective as feeding them their regular ration earlier in the day. Many competitors give their dogs an extra drink of baited or clear water in the evening to make up for the early feeding and to keep the dogs well hydrated. Mari often offers her dogs clear water after their evening meal, and she finds they will readily drink it without needing any flavoring. Tired dogs who turn down baited water often will drink clear water instead.

After the race, it's important to give the dogs a recovery snack or drink within twenty minutes after the run. There are a number of good products on the market designed to replenish your dog's energy stores.

Pre-Race Checkup

Be sure your dogs are healthy before you hook them up on race day. It's easy to be distracted by waxing your skis, checking over your gear, and setting up your pulk. Go over your dogs as carefully as you go over your equipment. Often, during Wednesday or Thursday training, you'll begin to see signs that indicate a dog won't perform well if you race him. You may not say a word to your team during your Wednesday run, but look closely at each dog. If one dog is a little bit down and

Water is often baited with kibble to make it more appetizing to tired dogs after a race.

you have a spare dog available, race with the spare—the dog that's down is not likely to recover enough in just two days.

Multiday Races

In a two- or three-day race, watch your dogs closely during the last two miles of each heat. Often, this is when you will see whom to take the next day. Sometimes your best dogs won't look as strong as some of the others when you go out, but when you put a little pressure on them coming home, they dig in. A weaker dog may have trouble with that pressure, and a dog that starts to fade will rarely improve on the second day.

Right after they come in from a race, check the dogs' feet for soreness or injuries and note the dogs' general condition. Give them a recovery snack within twenty minutes after the run. It's best to feed them fairly quickly after the day's competition is over so that they run on a relatively empty stomach the following day. Wait for an hour or so after the race so they can cool down and relax, but not much longer than three or four hours.

A good massage before and after each heat of a race will do wonders for a dog's sore muscles. Likewise, if you are able to loose-drop your dogs after each heat, they'll have a chance to stretch out and cool off, and you can evaluate their condition as they run around.

If you want an optimum performance on the second day of the race, always take care of your dogs first, before you go out to dinner or engage in long conversations with your competitors. It's a good idea to immediately write down or tell your partner if you have a dog that shouldn't go the next day. It's too easy to talk yourself into taking a problem dog as you talk the evening away.

Traveling Tips

Traveling should be a fun experience for your dogs. To keep them happy and healthy, provide them with daily exercise, a regular and predictable feeding schedule, and clean, dry boxes or kennels. For most dogs, travel is a break in the daily routine, a chance to see new trails, and a chance to have your undivided attention.

The following schedule works well for Mari when she's at a race in another area:

- Drop the dogs (let them out of their dog boxes or kennels) and give them baited water at eight a.m. Often they will do almost all of their pooping for the day if you can let them run around a bit after they drink.
- Drop the dogs again at ten a.m. to give them a chance to eliminate, and then allow them to rest in their boxes another hour or so before race or training time.

- After racing the dogs, feed and water them at around five p.m. Loose-drop them if you can. If you have a dog that seems a little sore, try a good massage. If it's more than just muscle soreness, this may be the time to decide whether to take that dog the next day.
- Drop them again two hours later.
- Drop one last time around nine or ten p.m. Then leave them alone so they can get a decent night's sleep. Mari's last drop is at nine p.m. so she and her dogs can sleep uninterrupted all night. Most of her dogs do well at that schedule, especially if they are loose-dropped.

Keep in mind that dogs don't rest as well in a moving vehicle. If you drive straight through to the race site, try to arrive early enough to give the dogs at least ten to twelve hours of rest before the race.

Organize your dog gear so that you can find it easily—being organized for a road trip is almost as important as being organized for a camping trip. To make storage easier, use nesting stainless steel or aluminum pans as dog dishes. Bread pans work well. Keep the gear in your truck clean, especially bowls and buckets.

Carol, who has a bad memory and lives by checklists, created a detailed list of gear and dog food for traveling to races, and she never leaves home without consulting it. There are few worse moments than arriving at a race hours from home, only to find you've forgotten a key piece of equipment. (During a multiday championship race in which she was running the four-dog class, Carol actually managed to forget her sled.)

A laundry can be a handy place to get warm water. Water the dogs with about a quart and a half of water each. After watering (and/or feeding), drop them once two hours afterward and again four hours afterward.

Keep an eye on the dogs' urine: clear urine is a sign of adequate hydration, but dark yellow urine may mean a lack of adequate fluids. Another way to test for hydration is to pull up the skin on the dog's neck. A dehydrated dog's skin loses its elasticity and won't immediately snap back to normal when released. Dry, sticky gums and lips, or sunken eyes, also indicate poor hydration.

Try to strike a balance between giving your dogs adequate amounts of water and going overboard—it's not necessary to drown your dogs in fluids when traveling. Remember, they can't get out of their boxes until you let them, and wet boxes aren't very comfortable.

If you have to leave your vehicle stationary and running at any time, be sure the exhaust can't filter into the dogs' boxes or kennels. Pay attention to the exhaust generated by other vehicles, too. Park away from other people and position your vehicle so that no one can park right next to you.

Drop your dogs where they won't cause a nuisance, and be absolutely meticulous in cleaning up after them. Train them to be quiet, especially at night. Whether you stay at a motel or with a fellow dog driver, you will quickly wear out your welcome—and every other dog driver's welcome—if your dogs bark all night long.

Mari's Suggested Training Calendar

This calendar is according to the climate of interior Alaska. Adjust specifics to the climate of your area. If you work at home, you'll be able to train more easily during the week. Those who squeeze in dog driving on top of a full-time job will want to use both Saturday and Sunday for training.

September

At the beginning of the fall season, you and your dog need to get back into shape. Start out slowly; consider how warm it is, and don't overheat yourself or your dog. Build up strength, endurance, and speed (in that order), but gradually. During bike or cart training, keep your speed under fifteen miles per hour at first.

Dryland racing in the fall can be both fun and good training. If you are aiming for the championships on snow, keep your long-term goals in sight.

Incorporate some obedience work in your training. Teach directions, stopping, passing. Early fall training is when you have the most control over the dog. On days off, let the dog run loose if you can, both to keep up his motivation and to strengthen the bond between you and your dog. Hunting and mountain trips are great both for strength training and for motivation and bonding.

Below are activities for a possible four-day training week, but many people can only train three days a week because of work schedules. Mari usually trains three times a week in September and October.

Tues: Run with dog (with skijoring line and belt),
        three to five miles. Or jog with dog loose.
Wed: Cart or bike training, three miles.
Fri: Run with dog, three to five miles.
Sun: Cart or bike training, three miles.

October

You and your dog should have built up a base of conditioning by now, so training can intensify. If you are using a cart, four-wheeler, or bike, increase your speed a little, to fifteen to sixteen miles per hour. To prevent injuries, build up endurance and strength *before* increasing speed. If possible, let your dogs run loose, or encourage them to run after toys or balls, to increase their speed on their own.

If you are lucky enough to have snow this early, start skiing by yourself often, with your dog loose if possible, to get back your balance and build up your own strength. Also continue to work on discipline and commands.

Tues: Run or skijor, five to eight miles.
Wed: Bike or cart, five miles.
Fri: Run or skijor, five to eight miles.
Sun: Bike or cart, five miles.

November

The Far North should have snow by now. If you'll be competing in Nordic-style races, introduce your dog to a weighted pulk with half the weight that will be used in competition. Stay on flat trails for this, and increase the weight as the month goes on. If you have more than two dogs, you can run them in front of a dogsled for variation.

Tues: Skijor eight to ten miles on groomed trails that have a variety of terrain.

Wed: Pulk training at slow speeds, five to ten miles depending on trail conditions.

Thurs: Skijor part of time, ski alone part of time with dog loose if possible. Fun day.

Sat: Pulk training same as Wednesday.

Sun: Skijor eight to ten miles or use sled.

December

Your dog should be able to maintain his basic speed for at least ten miles now. That means you also have to be in shape, because it's the teamwork that counts. A few races may start up, but continue training to concentrate on the races in February and March.

Tues: Skijor or use sled, twelve miles at an easy run.

Wed: Pulk training, using five to ten pounds more weight than competition for shorter distance, eight miles.

Thurs: Skijor ten to twelve miles, interval training—go five minutes at a fast pace and five minutes at a slow pace.

Sat/Sun: Races. If not, train with pulk one day, skijor the next, ten to twelve miles. Make sure you and your dog finish faster than you start out to accustom both of you to sprinting the last mile. Your dogs should come in stronger than they left.

January/February/March

You and your dog should be in race shape by now. It's important to maintain your conditioning. Overtraining may make your dog sour or lead to injuries, and can break down both the physical and mental condition of your dog. Rest is important. Give the dog a day off before one-day races and two days off before two-day races. Speed, motivation, and prevention of injuries are your top priorities. If possible, let the dog run loose sometimes to help maintain motivation.

Tues: Skijor, ten to twelve miles. If you have been loose-dropping and free-running your dogs, you do not need to train on Tuesday. Watch your team—overtraining at this point will cause injuries. This is the point at which you and your team should be peaking.

Wed: Skijor (or dogsled for variation), ten to twelve miles.

Sat/Sun: Races. If not, train with pulk one day (use race weight), skijor the next, ten to twelve miles.

April through August

April is a difficult month for the dogs. All of a sudden they're not running anymore. Now that Carol has run a couple of marathons, she wonders whether dogs get the same "taper crazies" that marathon runners do. Being in such good shape, with no outlet for all that strength and conditioning, can cause mood swings and hyperactivity in marathon runners, so why not also in working dogs? If it's possible to take a couple of recreational trips in the mountains, this is perfect timing. Such trips can be rewarding and are a pleasant way to end the season. It's also a good time to work with younger dogs, practice leader training, and let the activity level wind down gradually.

As you finish the race season, jot down or review your notes about the winter's training and racing before they fade from your memory. Write down any problems your dog had that might benefit from summer leash training, such as an erratic response to "on by" or some confusion with "gee" and "haw." Set your goals for the coming year and think of off-season activities that will further those goals. Remember to include both fun and challenging activities that will keep your dog in good mental and physical shape.

During the off season, it's helpful to work with your dogs two to three times a week. Remember that dogs need mental and physical breaks just as people do. If you have worked hard with your dog all winter, make the next few months a bit easier, a little more laid-back. Motivation is the most important priority in the summer. Take short runs with the dog in harness. Work on obedience or agility training. Some dedicated dog drivers have installed dog walkers or swimming pools for their dogs. Take your dogs swimming and

This pup is learning basic agility. Exposing young dogs to many different experiences makes them better skijoring dogs later on.

backpacking, and let them run loose (under supervision, of course) when possible. Focus on a mix of activities, and make sure that you pick at least a few that are strictly fun for your dog.

A Day at the Races

Here is what happens at a skijoring race put on by the Alaska Dog Mushers' Association (ADMA) in Fairbanks. Races in other areas may differ somewhat in the details, but many of the principles and procedures remain the same.

Race sign-up and drawing for position is usually held a few days before the weekend event. All race participants are required to be members of the organization holding the race; in this case, ADMA. This is common procedure and is often mandatory for liability insurance coverage. Some racers complain that they shouldn't have to purchase a club membership just to race in one event, but keep in mind that races don't happen by magic. Membership dues help cover the direct race costs of grooming the trail, photocopying time sheets, procuring bibs, purchasing paint for marking dogs (on multiday races), and drug-testing costs on championship races. Numerous indirect costs include soliciting sponsorships, maintaining a club building, insuring the events and the building, and handling the myriad other details required to administer a racing club.

At the drawing, take note of the scheduled race time, the time check-in closes on race day, the starting position you've drawn and the names of those going out just ahead of and behind you.

Arrival: On the day of the race, plan to be at the racegrounds in plenty of time (at least a half hour before the start time for your class). Even if you thrive on eleventh-hour deadlines, don't arrive late and rush around at the last minute. You personally may do well under such pressure, but it will upset your dogs. You will also drive race officials crazy if you always check in mere seconds before your class closes or appear at the starting line with only seconds to spare.

Check-in closes fifteen minutes before the race starts. It's best to check in early. At ADMA races, if you have not physically signed in before check-in closes, you are disqualified from that race. The race marshal is allowed to bend the rules for extenuating circumstances, but rarely does so. Don't count on it.

Check-in takes place at a check-in table inside the hall, where drivers are given a numbered bib. This is a good time to pick up a timesheet for your class. The check-in person can also tell you where to park and can let you know of any confirmed "scratches" (people who have withdrawn from the race).

Keep in mind that the check-in person is not empowered to make any decisions regarding the race, its rules, or its procedures. If you have a question about race rules or procedures, or if you wish to complain about a ruling, *don't* harass the check-in person. Go to the race marshal.

Prepare for the race by organizing your dogs, your equipment, and yourself. Remember: *No loose dogs!* No matter how well behaved they are.

Listen carefully to announcements. Sometimes a start time will change, often because someone scratched from a race. It helps to have your timesheet handy and to find out whether those in front of you are still planning to race.

Start intervals are usually two minutes apart, but ADMA has occasionally shortened the interval to one minute for skijorers and the smaller sled classes. Try not to hook up too early or too late. Keep track of which team is at the starting line. If the announcer doesn't tell you, watch for bib numbers or take note of where teams are parked in the holding area and track the one or two teams directly ahead of you. If a team scratches in front of you, you will move up to their spot, so keep on your toes and listen carefully for announcements.

Be ready to go when the team in front of you heads for the starting line. If, for example, your start position is number four in a race with two-minute intervals, you should start hooking up when number one is on the starting line. By the time number three heads up to the starting line, you and your team should be completely hooked up and ready to move.

If you are alone and need help getting your dogs to the starting line, ask somebody! Don't be shy. Most dog drivers and spectators are delighted to lend a hand and will jump to your assistance if they know you need it. For greater peace of mind, line up a handler before the race starts.

Once you get to the starting line, the tips of your skis determine the starting point of you and your dog(s). A "sled holder" (who may have a heck of a time figuring out how to hold a skijorer!) may be there to restrain you and your team if necessary, but be prepared to stop and hold your own team if the race is short on volunteers. The timer usually calls out warnings for two minutes to start, one minute, thirty seconds, and fifteen seconds, and then counts down five...four...three...two...one...GO!

DAVE PARTEE

Sometimes a little assistance is needed to get to the starting line.

If you have trouble getting off the starting line, you are allowed one handler to help you and your dogs out of the starting chute. Once you are past the chute, you are not allowed to accept any more help except from the turnaround marshal or other race officials empowered to help. Assistance is also permitted if a situation endangers you or the dogs. You are not permitted to have a handler help you through the finish chute.

You will be disqualified if you don't follow and complete the official race course or if you otherwise violate the race rules. Always ask for and *read* a current copy of the race rules. Pleading ignorance won't save you from disqualification if you commit a serious offense.

Cruel and inhumane treatment is grounds for being barred from future races. Take this rule seriously.

Follow the markers. The official ADMA race course is marked as follows: A red marker means an upcoming turn to the side of the trail where the marker is placed. (In other words, a red marker on the left warns of a turn to the left; a red marker on the right warns of a turn to the right.) A blue marker means the trail continues straight ahead. A yellow marker means use caution ahead. All turnarounds are marked with signs pointing to the turn and stating which turn it is; for example, 3.4 mile, 5.0 mile. If you can possibly do so, take your dogs around the official course at least once before the day of the race, so you and the dogs will be familiar with the trail.

Passing: If you overtake another driver and wish to pass, call "Trail!" loudly enough so that the driver ahead can hear. According to the race rules for skijoring, the other team is required to slow the dog(s) to the best of that driver's ability until you have passed, and the driver should leave enough room on the trail for you to get by. If you are passed, you have that same responsibility: to yield trail means to slow down or stop, to move your team over to one side, and to give the passing team an unobstructed path.

In the heat of competition, some people refuse to yield the trail. This is equivalent to shooting yourself in the foot. Not only will you hurt the other team's chances for a fast finish time, but *you will hurt your own time as well.* If you allow free, quick passage, your team will chase the team ahead of it (which is probably faster than yours or else it would not have caught you), and you will come in much faster than if you slow both teams down by obstructing the pass.

If the team that has been passed hangs on behind the passing team for a certain interval of time or distance (currently two and a half minutes or a half mile for skijorers), he or she can demand trail and repass. Keep in mind, however, that another way to sabotage the chances of both your team and your competitor's team is to tailgate the team that passes you. Most dogs hate to be tailgated; they look back nervously and often slow way down. You can't repass right away, and you want a fast chase, so it is to your advantage to give the passing team enough room to work back up to top speed. Even if your dogs keep up with the team ahead, it's probably wiser not to repass. Your dogs are chasing and likely will not sustain this speed if they are the lead team.

A team in the finishing chute does not have to yield the trail, nor must it wait to repass. But that does not mean you can't be gracious, and it does not give you license to engage in unsporting behavior.

The finish time is calculated when the first dog's nose crosses the finish line.

When you cross the finish line, move away from the finishing chute as quickly as possible. Don't hang around and cause traffic jams for other incoming or outgoing teams. Go immediately to your vehicle, secure your dogs, give them their recovery snack, and then turn in your bib as soon as possible.

Rest your dogs in a comfortable spot where they can lie down. In warm weather, you may want to give them a small drink and rest them in the shade if possible.

Always bring a shovel and container to clean up after your dogs. Be sure to clean up after yourself as well. People trash is as unwelcome as dog manure.

Thank race organizers! These people are volunteers who have given up part of their personal time (not to mention their sanity) to provide you with the opportunity to compete. Your words of thanks will mean more to them than you could imagine.

Don't forget to enjoy yourself, and to appreciate your dogs, as you race down the trail. If you are nervous or stressed out, your dogs may misbehave or may learn not to enjoy racing. If you are excited and happy while you are competing, your dogs will pick up on your mood and will run even better for you.

DAVE PARTEE

13

Where Can We Go From Here?

The Competitive Connection

When the first skijoring club in North America, the Alaska Skijoring and Pulk Association, formed in 1987, club members were divided into two factions: recreational and competitive. For the first year or two, these groups vied as opposing forces instead of uniting as complementary ones. Recreational skijorers, who constituted the vast majority of club members, felt the club emphasized racing too much and spent too much time organizing competitive events; racers, on the other hand, argued that competitions drew public interest and promoted the sport.

The conflict highlighted an important point. For better or worse, racing brings a sport into the public eye. It is difficult—though certainly not impossible—to make an "event" out of a recreational skijoring tour. A race, however, is an event by definition. People come to competitive events because they are exciting and fun to watch.

The element of winning adds dimension to the spectators' enjoyment. What would the Iditarod Sled Dog Race be like, in terms of public involvement and media coverage, if a bunch of dog mushers got together once a year to travel the old Iditarod trail just for fun, and it didn't matter who reached Nome first? Such an event actually exists, and it sometimes gets a tiny bit of local media coverage, but who other than local Alaskans has ever heard of it?

Although recreational dog mushers far outnumber those who compete, it is because of competitive mushing events that the public knows about the sport. We support and promote competitive skijoring events for this reason. In Alaska, where skijorers abound, only a relative handful compete in races. But those few bring the sport into the public eye and encourage more recreational sorts to hitch up the family pet. It's like an iceberg: competitive skijorers are the highly visible tip, bolstered by a vast unseen foundation of recreational skijorers.

Competition leads to other benefits as well. The drive to win often generates improvements in gear, breeding, or techniques that benefit all participants, not just racers. For example, the racing Alaskan husky, with its remarkable speed and endurance, is a

This 1898 photo of stampeders during the Klondike gold rush shows old-style harnesses and traces in a single-file hitch. Racing has fostered many technological advances in equipment.

product of selective breeding by dog-mushing competitors. These wonderful dogs are used by most recreational mushers as well. Competitive skijorers in Fairbanks have come up with several beneficial innovations in gear over the years. Two early innovations were major improvements that are now considered standard. Weaving a section of bungee into the core of the skijoring line replaced the old method of attaching an external bungee to the line. And leg straps have been added to many skijoring belts to keep them from riding up in back. All skijorers, recreational as well as competitive, now benefit from these innovations.

Competition-quality dog food is another excellent example of an improvement born of racing but valuable to all dog drivers. The increased popularity of long-distance races such as the Iditarod and Yukon Quest, along with the intense competition among sprint mushers, led several companies to make major improvements in their commercial dog food. Because of competitive dog mushing, a recreational musher now can purchase a nutritionally complete feed for his sled dogs, instead of being forced to settle for something less or to make up his own diet.

Certainly recreational skijorers will always outnumber competitors. But it is the skijoring races that have sprung up across North America that will expose more people to the idea that they can dust off their skis, harness up their resident couch-potato pooch, and have a wonderful time.

Where Is the Sport Going?

In 1991, when *Skijor With Your Dog* was first published, skijoring was often viewed as a lowly stepchild by both Alaska-style and Nordic-style dog mushers. It was not a *real* sport, just a training technique or a backyard sort of activity, with no competitive merit. Nearly ten years later, when the International Federation of Sleddog Sports began planning for its 2001 World Championships (the musher's equivalent of the Olympics) to be held in Fairbanks,

Carol spearheaded an audacious proposal to include skijoring as a regular competitive class. The fight was long and hard, the discussions lengthy and often heated. Many organizers felt skijoring was not an appropriate class for these elite races and should only be a demonstration sport. But finally, with the support of the skijoring club in Fairbanks plus the backing of Kathy Frost and several other top competitive mushers, the skijorers won their battle and skijoring was added as a bona fide competitive class.

From its humble beginnings, skijoring now is a regular class in the IFSS World Championships and a sanctioned class with the International Sled Dog Racing Association in North America. Races abound all over North America and have caught on in Europe as well. The "backyard" sport has come into its own as a legitimate competitive activity, and its popularity continues to grow.

Ultimately, we think skijoring has the potential to surpass *both* Alaska-style and Nordic-style dog driving in visibility and popularity. The reason is simple math: Add up the number of recreational cross-country skiers worldwide who own a dog. Big number. Then try to figure out how many people around the globe have the time, money, room, and zoning for a large kennel of dogs. Not such a big number. The pool of potential skijorers is therefore greater than that of potential dog mushers. At least, that's our theory. And our hope is that skijoring, as a former stepchild of both Alaskan- and Nordic-style mushing, may become the link that unites dog drivers around the world.

Future Skijoring Races

Many skijoring races in the United States are short ones of three to five miles. We feel race organizers should consider adding longer races to their events as well. Short mileages help to attract newcomers into the sport, but a three-mile run doesn't test the skill and endurance of either skier or dog. Skijoring will likely gain credibility among more elite athletes with longer mileage that shows the dogs—and their drivers—can easily handle the extra miles.

The focus of Nordic-style competition in Europe has been the teamwork between the skier and the dog—the dog must pull a significant amount of weight, and the skier must be in excellent condition. European pulk racers who came to Winnipeg, Canada, for the 1991 International Federation of Sleddog Sports World Championship Sled Dog Races were displeased with the short (six-and-a-half-mile), flat course. They wanted longer mileage and more hills!

There is logic to this viewpoint. On a flat trail, the skier with more dogs enjoys a distinct advantage, even though the pulks are weighted, because once the dogs get up their momentum, each dog can maintain a high speed without pulling as hard. On a hilly trail, a one-dog team can beat a three-dog team; the hills equalize the dog power and top skiing skills make the difference. Likewise, speed is everything on a short skijoring trail. On a longer trail, the endurance and conditioning of both dog and skier will play a much larger part.

The Olympics?

For at least eighty years, dog drivers have dreamed of seeing their sport added to the Olympics. Skijoring, although behind horses instead of dogs, was a demonstration sport at the 1928 Winter Olympics in St. Moritz, Switzerland. An Alaska-style dog-mushing demonstration race was held at the 1932 Winter Olympics at Lake Placid, New York, and a Nordic-style exhibition was held at the 1952 Winter Olympics in Oslo, Norway. So far, no dog-driving sport has been adopted.

The Olympics includes equine competition; why not canine as well? Could it be because there are so many more equine competitions than dog-driving competitions overall? Or because

equine competitions are considered more elite, and dog mushing too proletarian?

The International Federation of Sleddog Sports has been working for many years toward inclusion of a dog-driving event at the Olympics. Perhaps what is needed is a groundswell of public support, along with increased visibility for dog drivers. Skijoring, with its broad base of potential participants, could help to swing the vote. This has been, and continues to be, our dream.

Whether or not this lofty dream of Olympic skijoring comes true some day, we hope more and more people catch the skijoring fever. Every skijorer, on every trail and in every race, is an ambassador for our sport and a key to its future.

Because It's Really the Dogs

Skijoring races are fun, exciting, and challenging; but so are stock-car races, skydiving, and raising kids. Racing is only one small aspect of the sport of skijoring. For most of us who own pulling dogs, it is the dogs themselves that make the activity worthwhile. Downhill skiing is fast, and cross-country skiing is great exercise. Many of us love simply being outdoors on a snowy trail. Add a dog, and somehow you've added much more than a little extra power. You've added a companion, a partner, and a whole new perspective. You often see the trail through new eyes, trying to imagine what the dog sees. A hard-pulling dog gives you a feeling of power and speed that is indescribable. As you ski down a silent, snow-covered trail behind your dog in harness, you are engaged in a shared activity that connects you at a deeper level than simple companionship might.

As skijorers, we work with our dogs, learn to communicate effectively with them, teach them how to pull us, and best of all, nurture the incredible joy of running that most dogs were born with. In the process of harnessing that joy, we experience it ourselves.

DAVE PARTEE

Resources

The list of skijoring resources changes constantly. On the Web, search the word "skijor" or "skijoring." Many skijoring and sled groups have Facebook pages. You can find this book on Facebook, too (https://www.facebook.com/skijorwithyourdog).

Skijoring equipment outfitters were once hard to find, but no more. On the Web, search "skijor equipment," check out the "Equipment & Supplies" page at Sled Dog Central, or find vendors through dog-driving magazines (see below).

E-mail Lists and Groups

Alaska Skijoring and Pulk Association: Join at http://groups
  .yahoo.com/group/Skijoring/
SDC Talk! (Sled Dog Central forum): Join at http://www
  .sleddogcentral.com/forum/
Skidogs.ca forum: Join at http://www.skidogs.ca/Forum/
Skijor forum: Join at http://groups.yahoo.com/group/SKIJOR
  / and, to find other skijor groups at Yahoo! Groups (http://
  groups.yahoo.com), search the word "skijor."
Sleddog-L: Send an e-mail with the words **subscribe sleddog-l**
  to **listserv@apple.ease.lsoft.com**, with no subject line.

Selected Skijoring Clubs and Organizations

Below are a few of the skijoring organizations in North America. Many sled dog clubs include skijoring at their races and other events. See the "Skijor & Pulka" column in Sled Dog Central's race schedule for details (http://www.sleddogcentral.com /schedules/race_schedules.htm).

Alaska Skijoring and Pulk Association

P.O. Box 82843
Fairbanks, AK 99708-2843 USA
907-457-5456 (hotline)
http://www.alaskaskijoring.org
info@alaskaskijoring.org
Facebook: https://www.facebook.com/pages
/Alaska-Skijoring-Pulk-Association/116958338411282

Anchorage Skijor Club

P.O. Box 240573
Anchorage, AK 99524 USA
907-349-9663 (event updates)
http://skijoring.org
Facebook: https://www.facebook.com/pages
/Anchorage-Skijor-Club/152081628151255

Midwest Skijorers Club

Blaine, MN 55434 USA
763-218-5956
http://www.skijor.org
midwestskijorers@comcast.net
Facebook: https://www.facebook.com
/groups/50995864766/

Pacific Sled Dog and Skijor Association

> Membership: William Reid, Treasurer
> 14624 Piney Court
> Klamath Falls, OR 97601 USA
> http://www.psdsa.org

Skidogs.ca

> http://www.skidogs.ca

Skijor USA

> http://www.skijorusa.org
> Facebook: https://www.facebook.com
> /groups/161519457212980/

Skijoring (Facebook group)

> https://www.facebook.com/group
> .php?gid=8359239123&v=wall

International Sled Dog Organizations

European Canicross Federation

> http://www.cani-cross.eu/website/

European Sled Dog Racing Association (ESDRA)

> http://www.esdra.net

International Federation of Sleddog Sports (IFSS)

> http://sleddogsport.net/

International Sled Dog Racing Association (ISDRA)

> 22702 Rebel Road
> Merrifield, MN 56465 USA
> http://www.isdra.org

International Sled Dog Veterinary Medical Association (ISDVMA)

P.O. Box 828
Putney, VT 05346 USA
http://www.isdvma.org
Facebook: https://www.facebook.com/pages
/ISDVMA/108940862479098

Mushing USA

http://www.mushingusa.org

Selected North American Dog-Driving Publications

Dog & Driver magazine

22702 Rebel Road
Merrifield, MN 56465 USA
http://www.isdra.org

Mushing magazine

Box 1195
Willow, AK 99688 USA
907-495-2468
http://www.mushing.com

Sled Dog Welfare Organization

Mush with P.R.I.D.E.

P.O. Box 1915
Kenai, AK 99611 USA
907-490-6874 (messages)
http://www.mushwithpride.org
info@mushwithpride.org

Glossary

Airline kennel: A small kennel designed to transport dogs on airplanes. Also known as a *sky kennel.*

Alaskan husky: A nonstandard breed of sled dog developed for its speed, drive, and stamina. Bred for performance. Appearance may vary widely. May be a mix of husky (such as Siberian) and non-northern breeds, such as pointer, hound, or retriever. Not recognized by the American Kennel Club.

Alaska-style dog mushing: Three to twenty dogs, usually in sets of two, pull a dogsled ridden by the driver. See also *Nome-style dog mushing.*

Anorak: A type of cold-weather jacket with a hood, often pullover style. Light, windproof anoraks are sometimes used as the outermost clothing layer for skiing.

Baited water: Water to which flavoring, such as leftover dog food, meat, or broth, has been added to make it more appealing.

Belly band: A band that attaches to the sides of a harness and runs under the dog's belly, used to prevent the dog from backing out of the harness.

Belly blanket: A covering that can be worn underneath a dog's harness to protect its belly.

Bikejoring: Being pulled on a bike by a dog in harness.

Bootie: A socklike covering that goes over the dog's foot and is fastened at the wrist or ankle to protect the dog's feet.

Breastplate: The part of a dog harness that covers the dog's breastbone (sternum) between the front legs.

Bridle: Rope rigging on a sled (such as a dogsled or a little plastic sled) to which the dog's tugline or a gangline is attached.

Bungee: An elastic cord designed to absorb variable pulling forces by stretching and contracting. Also known as *shock cord*.

Burn out: To push a working dog too hard, to the point where the dog becomes unwilling to pull or incapable of performing at maximum.

Canicross: Running on foot while being pulled by a dog in harness.

Carabiner: An oblong metal ring used to connect lines. Locking carabiners have a threaded section that secures the carabiner in the closed position.

Chute or **start chute**: The beginning portion of a race trail, usually bordered by fencing or other marking material, to keep teams on (and spectators off) the trail.

Climbing harness: A harness worn around a person's hips and legs, used in rock climbing. Usually made of open webbing.

"Come around": Command to reverse direction.

"Come gee" or **"Come haw"**: Command to reverse direction by coming back to the right or the left.

Command leader: A lead dog trained to obey directional commands. A lead dog that runs in front of a team but does not know directional commands is sometimes referred to as a "trail leader." See also *Gee-haw leader*.

Conformation: The physical structure or form of a dog, based on its bone structure and muscle placement.

Crotch band: A cloth covering worn at the dog's hindquarters to protect the genitals from freezing.

Dehydration: An abnormally low level of body fluids caused by inadequate intake of liquids or by excessive loss of fluids through sweating, diarrhea, vomiting, etc.

Dewclaw: The vestigial toe and claw located on the inside of each front leg above the dog's pads.

Diagonal striding: In cross-country skiing, the technique of gliding straight forward on one ski, then shifting weight and gliding forward on the other ski.

Dipping snow: A habit some dogs acquire of biting mouthfuls of snow while running.

Diuretic: A tendency to increase the flow of urine.

Dog boxes or **dog hauler**: A structure used to transport multiple dogs, consisting of a series of individual compartments placed on the back of a pickup or, occasionally, on a trailer. "Dog box" in common use may refer to either the hauler or to the individual box.

Dog coat: A blanket-style covering that can be worn under or over the dog's harness.

Dog musher: One who drives a team of dogs in harness. Also known as "dog driver."

Dog yard: An area where multiple dogs are tethered out or kenneled.

Dogsled: A type of sled used in Alaska-style dog mushing.

Double lead: Running two lead dogs side by side. Can also refer to the set of double tuglines used to hitch up two leaders.

Double poling: Planting and then pulling back on both poles at once to propel the skier forward.

Drag: A piece of trail-grooming equipment, usually made of metal or wood, that smoothes out and packs down the surface of the trail.

Drop chain or **drop line**: A short length of chain with snaps at both ends, used to attach a dog to a vehicle on a short-term basis.

Dryland mushing, dryland skijoring, or **dryland sports**: Inclusive terms for various forms of dog driving on dry ground rather than on snow.

"Easy": Command to reduce speed or power.

Fan hitch or **fan-style hitch**: Running three or more dogs abreast of one another.

Fid: A sturdy, hollow pin used in weaving rope.

Fieldwork: Training a dog for hunting.

Gait: The manner in which a dog moves forward at a walk, trot, or lope.

Gaiter: Protective cloth or leather leg covering that reaches from the instep of the foot to the mid-calf or knee. Used to increase warmth, break the wind, and keep snow out of a skier's or hiker's boot.

Gangline: A section of poly rope designed for use in running dog teams of three or more. The gangline consists of a main centerline, also known as a "towline," to which are attached tuglines and necklines.

"Gee": Command to turn right.

Gee-haw leader: A lead dog trained to turn right or left on command. See also *Command leader*.

"Gee over": Command to move over to the right.

Gee pole: A steering pole that extends forward from the right side of a dogsled.

Gig: A wheeled cart or rig designed to be pulled on dry ground by a dog or dogs in harness.

Groomed trail: A trail that has been broken out and smoothed down by snowmachine, drag, and/or track-setting machinery.

Guard hairs: The long outer hairs that protect a dog's undercoat.

Handler: An assistant who may help a dog driver with such tasks as hooking up dogs, doing dog yard chores, training teams, caring for the dogs when traveling, or working with puppies.

Harness breaking: Teaching a dog how to pull in harness.

"Haw": Command to turn left.

"Haw over": Command to move over to the left.

H-back harness: A dog harness with straps that form an H over the dog's back.

"Hike": Command to the dogs to begin pulling or to increase speed.

Holding area: The area at a race or dedicated dog-mushing track where vehicles are parked and dogs are harnessed up before a run.

Hound: A type of hunting dog often bred into husky lines. Some dog drivers use the term "hound" as a nonspecific term referring to non-northern breeds. See also *Pointer.*

Hound cross: A dog crossbred from hound and husky lines. Often used as a generic term that includes pointer cross. See also *Pointer cross.*

Husky: Generic term for northern-breed sled dogs, including both mixed breeds and purebreds.

Hypothermic: Having an abnormally low body temperature.

Ice hook: A type of brake used in Alaska-style dog mushing. Generally has sharpened points that can be driven into ice. See also *Snow hook.*

Interval training: Alternating intervals of top speeds with intervals of slower speeds. Used to increase speed and aerobic capacity.

Kennel: In dog mushing, a group of dogs kept for the purpose of mushing or skijoring.

Kickbike or **kick scooter**: See *Scooter.*

Lapp turn: Reversing direction on skis by lifting one ski at a time and turning it 180 degrees.

Lead dog or **leader**: The dog that runs in front of the team. Usually one that takes directional commands.

"Line out": Command to hold team out and keep the dog's tug-line tight.

Limited or **limited class**: A race or class within a race in which the size of the dog team is limited to a specific number of dogs; e.g., two-dog skijoring class.

Mass start: A type of race start where all competitors in a class begin at the same moment, typically in a wide area that eventually funnels down into a normal race trail.

Metabolism: The set of chemical reactions and processes that happen in the cells of a dog or person to convert energy and sustain life.

Mogul: A large bump in a trail, often created by high-speed snowmachines.

Mush: To run a team of dogs in harness. "Mush" is almost never used as a command for a team to begin pulling.

Musher: A dog driver. See also *Dog musher*.

Neckline: A short length of line that runs from the dog's collar to a gangline or to another dog, used to keep the dog from turning around or running out to the side.

Necklining: Refers to a dog pulling back against the neckline, usually either in protest or if incapable of maintaining the same speed as the rest of the team.

Nome-style dog mushing: A term used in Europe to describe the type of dog mushing most common in North America. See also *Alaska-style dog mushing*.

Nordic-style dog mushing: Skiing behind a pulk that is pulled by a dog or dogs in harness.

Obedience work: A catch-all term for teaching a dog obedience commands such as "sit," "stay," "come," "lie down," and "heel."

"On by": Command to go past a distraction or turn. See also *Straight ahead*.

Open class: A class of race in which the number of dogs per team is not limited. Usually used in a sprint-racing context. Also known as "unlimited class."

Overflow: Water from a stream, river, or lake that seeps up and floods the surface of snow or ice.

Pace: The speed at which a team or dog travels; also, a gait similar to the trot but in which the dog's front and rear legs on each side move forward and backward together, rather than diagonally as in a trot.

Panic snap: See *Quick-release snap*.

Pedaling: In Alaska-style mushing, standing on a sled runner with one foot and pushing off with the other foot. Also used when being pulled on a scooter or kickbike.

Picket or **picket line**: A length of chain or cable with shorter chain or cable lines attached at regular intervals for individual dogs. Used to secure multiple dogs.

Pointer: A type of hunting dog that is often bred into husky lines. See also *Hound*.

Pointer cross: A dog crossbred from pointer and husky lines. See also *Hound cross*.

Polypropylene rope: A type of woven, hollow synthetic line commonly used in dog mushing. Tuglines, ganglines, and necklines are often constructed of this rope. Also known as "poly rope."

Pulk or **pulka**: A small, narrow sled designed to be pulled by a dog or skier.

Pup: A working sled dog younger than a year old.

Quick link: A piece of hardware in the shape of a chain link, used as a connecting link on chains or lines.

Quick-release snap: A snap that releases when its outer casing is pulled backward. Designed to be released easily even by a mittened hand.

Race marshal: The official who monitors compliance with race rules.

Racing harness: A dog harness constructed of lightweight webbing, designed for efficient pulling at a fast pace or over long distances.

Rig: A wheeled cart designed to be pulled by one or more dogs in harness. See also *Gig*.

Rollerjoring: Being pulled on roller skates or roller skis by a dog in harness.

S-hook: An S-shaped metal piece used to connect chain links or swivels.

Scooter: A two-wheeled rig that allows the rider to pedal with one foot on the ground. Also known as a *Kickbike* or *Kick scooter*.

Shock cord: See *Bungee*.

Sidehill: Refers to the side of a slope or a trail that runs along the side of a hill rather than straight up or straight down the hillside.

Single lead: A dog that runs alone in the front of a team.

Skating: In cross-country skiing, moving forward on skis by means of a skating stroke.

Ski-boot covers: Covers that slip over ski boots to increase warmth and cut down on windchill.

Skijoring: Being pulled on skis by a dog in harness.

Skijoring belt: An extra-wide belt (at least three inches wide across the back) with a quick-release snap or open hook on the front that attaches to a skijoring line.

Skijoring line: The line that connects a skijorer to a dog, with a loop at one end to hook to the skijorer's belt and a snap at the other end that attaches to the dog's harness. Includes a section of bungee.

Ski touring: Taking day or overnight trips on skis.

Sky kennel: See *Airline kennel*.

Sled dog: A dog trained to pull a sled or skier. Sometimes used to describe northern-breed pulling dogs in general.

Snowballs: In dog mushing, the clumps of snow that sometimes form in between the pads of a dog's foot.

Snow hook: A metal brake, usually with two prongs, that is placed by hand into the snow to stop and hold a dog team. See also *Ice hook*.

Snowplowing: Angling ski tips together and tails outward in a V formation to slow the skier's speed.

Snub line: A line used to anchor a team to a post or tree while hooking up.

Sour: Used to describe a dog that has become discouraged about pulling through improper training, overtraining, stress, a bad or frightening experience, poor nutrition, or other factors.

Split: A fissure or crack in the pad or webbing of the foot.

Spooky: Used to describe a dog that frightens easily or is shy with humans or unfamiliar objects.

Sprint race: A shorter race, usually three to thirty miles, in which the dogs lope at a fast pace.

Star turn: Turning on skis by stepping around in a circle.

Starting chute: The area of a racetrack or trail where competitive teams begin the race. Often fenced or blocked off to keep dogs on course and spectators off the trail.

"Straight ahead": Command to go straight ahead at an intersection or to go by a distraction. See also *On by.*

Swivel: A two-piece connecting section of hardware that allows a chain or snap to twist around without binding up.

Tandem hitch: Running a team of dogs in a line of pairs rather than in a fan hitch. In the early days of mushing, the term referred to dogs in single file, a technique still used sometimes on narrow trails.

Tie-out chain: A length of chain designed to secure a dog. Often includes a quick link or snap at one end that attaches to a stake or other immovable object, a swivel in the middle of the chain, and a snap at the other end that attaches to the dog's collar. Also known as a "stake-out chain."

"Trail": A signal from a dog driver who is overtaking another team and wishes to pass.

Trailhead: The starting point of a trail.

Tugline: The section of line that attaches the dog's harness to the main skijoring line or gangline.

Two-dog lead: The section of line used to attach two lead dogs in a team.

Undercoat: The layer of fur next to the dog's skin.

Urban mushing: Inclusive term for dog-driving activities in densely populated areas.

Vetrap: A brand name for a stretchy bandage material that adheres to itself.

Waist pack: A small pack worn on a belt around a skier's or hiker's waist.

"Walk": Command to walk forward without pulling.

Webbing: The skin between a dog's toes. Also, narrow strips of material, often nylon or a nylon blend, used in making dog harnesses or climbing harnesses and occasionally used as a component of skijoring belts.

Weight-pulling harness: A type of dog harness specially designed for pulling heavy weights. Generally unsuitable for skijoring or dog mushing.

Wheel: The position directly in front of the skier or sled in a multidog team.

Wheel dog: The dog that runs in the position closest to the skier or sled in a multidog team.

"Whoa": Command to stop.

Working dog: A dog that is expected to perform a specific functional task, such as pulling, tracking, herding, hunting, or retrieving.

X-back harness: The most common type of Alaska-style mushing harness, with straps that cross over to form an X on the back of the dog.

Yearling: A dog in its first year after puppyhood. Puppies are often born in the summer and are referred to as "pups" for the first winter season following their birth. During their second winter season, when they are either just under or just over a year old, they are referred to as "yearlings."

Bibliography

Some books are listed under more than one heading.

Behavior

Bradshaw, John. *Dog Sense: How the New Science of Dog Behavior Can Make You a Better Friend to Your Pet.* New York: Basic Books, 2011.

Clothier, Suzanne. *Bones Would Rain from the Sky: Deepening Our Relationships with Dogs.* New York: Warner Books, 2002.

Collins, Sophie. *Tail Talk: Understanding the Secret Language of Dogs.* San Francisco: Chronicle Books, 2007.

Coppinger, Ray, and Lorna Coppinger. *Dogs: A New Understanding of Canine Origin, Behavior and Evolution.* Chicago: University of Chicago Press, 2002.

Coren, Stanley. *How Dogs Think: Understanding the Canine Mind.* New York: Free Press, 2004.

Fogle, Bruce. *The Dog's Mind: Understanding Your Dog's Behavior.* London: Pelham Books, 1990.

Grandin, Temple, and Catherine Johnson. *Animals Make Us Human.* Boston: Mariner Books, 2009.

McConnell, Patricia B. *The Other End of the Leash: Why We Do What We Do Around Dogs.* New York: Ballantine Books, 2002.

———. *For the Love of a Dog: Understanding Emotion in You and Your Best Friend.* New York: Ballantine Books, 2007.

Mech, David L., and Luigi Boitani, eds. *Wolves: Behavior, Ecology and Conservation.* Chicago: University of Chicago Press, 2003.

Breeding and Rearing Dogs

Bailey, Gwen. *The Perfect Puppy: How to Raise a Well-Behaved Dog.* New York: Reader's Digest, 2009.

Conn, Jeff. *Open North American Pedigree Books.* Ester, AK: Jeff Conn, multiple years (published annually).

Coppinger, Ray, and Lorna Coppinger. *Dogs: A New Understanding of Canine Origin, Behavior and Evolution.* Chicago: University of Chicago Press, 2002.

Dunbar, Ian. *Before and After Getting Your Puppy: The Positive Approach to Raising a Happy, Healthy, and Well-Behaved Dog.* Novato, CA: New World Library, 2004.

Holst, Phyllis A. *Canine Reproduction: A Breeder's Guide.* 2nd ed. Loveland, CO: Alpine Publications, 2000.

Isabell, Jackie. *Genetics: An Introduction for Dog Breeders.* Loveland, CO: Alpine Publications, 2002.

Rutherford, Clarice, and David H. Neil. *How to Raise a Puppy You Can Live With.* Rev. ed. Loveland, CO: Alpine Publications, 2005.

Conformation and Gait

Brown, Curtis M. *Dog Locomotion and Gait Analysis.* Wheat Ridge, CO: Hoflin Publishers, 1986.

Elliot, Rachel Page. *Dogsteps: A New Look.* 3rd ed. Irvine, CA: Doral Publishing, 2001.

Gilbert, Edward M. Jr., and Thelma R. Brown. *K-9 Structure & Terminology.* Wenatchee, WA: Dogwise Publishing, 2001.

Hollenbeck, Leon. *The Dynamics of Canine Gait.* Akron, NY: Hollenbeck, 1971.

Smythe, R. H. *Dog Structure and Movement.* New York: Arco Publishing, 1970.

Dog Driving

Some of these books are out of print but may be available at libraries or used-book sellers.

Attla, George, and Bella Levorsen. *Everything I Know About Training and Racing Sled Dogs.* Rome, NY: Arner Publications, 1974.

Cary, Bob, and Gail de Marcken. *Born to Pull: The Glory of Sled Dogs.* Minneapolis: University of Minnesota Press, 2009.

Collins, Miki, and Julie Collins. *Dog Driver: A Guide for the Serious Musher.* 2nd ed. Loveland, CO: Alpine Publications, 2009.

Coppinger, Lorna, with the International Sled Dog Racing Association. *The World of Sled Dogs: From Siberia to Sport Racing.* New York: Howell Book House, 1982.

Cowan, Nancy. *The Training and Racing Journals of Roland and Louise Lombard.* Deering, NH: Nancy Cowan, 2004.

Dogs of the North. Anchorage: Alaska Geographic, 1987.

Fishback, Lee. *Training Lead Dogs.* Nunica, MI: Tun-Dra, 1978.

Fishback, Lee, and Mel Fishback. *Novice Sled Dog Training.* Alderwood Manor, WA: Raymond Thompson, 1961.

Flanders, Noël K. *The Joy of Running Sled Dogs.* Loveland, CO: Alpine Publications, 1989.

Haakenstad, Matt, and John Thompson. *Ski Spot Run.* Minnetonka, MN: KISATI Ventures, 2004.

Harding, Jessie, and Raymond Thompson. *Skijoring with Dogs.* Lynnwood, WA: Raymond Thompson Company, 1982.

Kaynor, Carol, and Mari Høe-Raitto. *Skijoring: An Introduction to the Sport.* Fairbanks: Kaynor and Høe-Raitto, 1988.

LaBelle, Charlene, ed., for the Sierra Nevada Dog Drivers. *MUSH! A Beginner's Manual of Sled Dog Training.* 4th ed. Mechanicsburg, PA: Barkleigh Productions, 2007.

Mush with P.R.I.D.E. *Sled Dog Care Guidelines.* 3rd ed. Kenai, AK: Mush with P.R.I.D.E., 2009.

Riddles, Libby, and Tim Jones. *Race Across Alaska.* Harrisburg, PA: Stackpole Books, 1988.

Schmidt, Karin E. *The Musher & Veterinarian Handbook.* 2nd ed. Putney, VT: ISDVMA, 2001.

Shields, Mary. *Sled Dog Trails.* Anchorage: Alaska Northwest Publishing Company, 1984.

Turner, A. Allan, ed. *The Iditarod Arctic Sports Medicine/Human Performance Guide.* Anchorage: Alaska Regional Chapter of the American College of Sports Medicine, 1988.

U.S. War Department. *Dog Transportation.* Taylors Falls, MN: Taylors Falls Bookstore Publication, 1944.

Vaudrin, Bill, ed. *Racing Alaskan Sled Dogs.* Anchorage: Alaska Northwest Publishing, 1976.

Welch, Jim. *The Speed Mushing Manual: How to Train Racing Sled Dogs.* Eagle River, AK: Sirius Publishing, 1989.

General

American Kennel Club. *The Complete Dog Book.* 20th ed. New York: Ballantine Books, 2006.

Caras, Roger. *A Celebration of Dogs.* New York: Times Books, 1982.

Clothier, Suzanne. *Bones Would Rain from the Sky: Deepening Our Relationships with Dogs.* New York: Warner Books, 2002.

Fogle, Bruce. *The New Encyclopedia of the Dog.* 2nd ed. New York: Dorling Kindersley, 2001.

Hearne, Vicki. *Adam's Task: Calling Animals by Name.* New York: Vintage Books, 1987.

Serpell, James. *In the Company of Animals.* New York: Basil Blackwell, 1986.

Health and Nutrition

Ackerman, Lowell. *Skin and Haircoat Problems in Dogs.* Loveland, CO: Alpine Publications, 1994.

Bower, John, and David Youngs. *The Health of Your Dog.* Loveland, CO: Alpine Publications, 1989.

Eldredge, Debra M., Liisa D. Carlson, Delbert G. Carlson, and James M. Giffin. *The Dog Owner's Home Veterinary Handbook.* 4th ed. New York: Howell Book House, 2007.

Grandjean, Dominique, Nathalie Moquet, Sandrine Pawlowiez, Anne-Karen Tourtebatte, Boris Jean, and Hélène Bacqué. *Practical Guide for Sporting and Working Dogs.* Aimargues, France: Royal Canin, 2000.

Gustafson, Sid. *First Aid for the Active Dog.* Loveland, CO: Alpine Publications, 2003.

Kahn, Cynthia M., and Scott Line, eds. *The Merck Veterinary Manual.* 10th ed. Whitehouse Station, NJ: Merck & Co., 2010.

Redding, Richard W., and Myrna L. Papurt. *The Dog's Drugstore.* New York: St. Martin's Press, 2000.

Snow, Amy, and Nancy Zidonis. *The Well-Connected Dog.* Larkspur, CO: Tallgrass Publishers, 1999.

USDA Natural Resources Conservation Service. *Composting Dog Waste.* Washington, DC: USDA, 2005.

Zink, M. Christine. *Dog Health & Nutrition for Dummies.* New York: Wiley Publishing, 2001.

Training, General

Burnham, Patricia Gail. *Playtraining Your Dog.* New York: St. Martin's Press, 1980.

Campbell, William E. *Owner's Guide to Better Behavior in Dogs.* 2nd ed. Loveland, CO: Alpine Blue Ribbon Books, 1995.

Dunbar, Ian. *Dog Behavior: An Owner's Guide to a Happy, Healthy Pet.* New York: Howell Book House, 1996.

McConnell, Patricia B., and Karen London. *Feisty Fido.* Black Earth, WI: Dog's Best Friend, 2003.

McGreevy, Paul, and Robert A. Boakes. *Carrots and Sticks: Principles of Animal Training.* Cambridge: Cambridge University Press, 2008.

Monks of New Skete. *How to Be Your Dog's Best Friend: A Training Manual for Dog Owners.* Rev. ed. Boston: Little, Brown, 2002.

Pryor, Karen. *Don't Shoot the Dog! The New Art of Teaching and Training.* Rev. ed. New York: Bantam, 1999.

Rutherford, Clarice, and David H. Neil. *How to Raise a Puppy You Can Live With.* Rev. ed. Loveland, CO: Alpine Publications, 2005.

Volhard, Jack, and Wendy Volhard. *Dog Training for Dummies.* New York: Wiley Publishing, 2005.

Zink, M. Christine. *Peak Performance: Coaching the Canine Athlete.* 2nd ed. Lutherville, MD: Canine Sports Productions, 1999.

Winter Camping

Barve, Betty. *Dog Mushers Trail Food and Old Fashion Recipe Book.* Wasilla, AK: L&B Color Printing, 1989.

Bridge, Raymond. *The Complete Snow Camper's Guide.* Mountain View, CA: World Publications, 1973.

Danielson, John. *Winter Hiking and Camping.* Mountain View, CA: World Publications, 1972.

Gorman, Stephen. *The Winter Camping Handbook: Wilderness Travel & Adventure in the Cold-Weather Months.* Woodstock, VT: Countryman Press, 2007.

Nordic World Magazine: Snow Camping Guide. Mountain View, CA: World Publications, 1980.

Pilon, André. *The Universe of Sled Dogs.* Montmagny, Québec: Edition Marquis Ltd., 1999.

Rutstrum, Calvin. *Paradise Below Zero.* Mountain View, CA: World Publications, 1968.

Tilton, Buck, and John Gookin. *National Outdoor Leadership School Winter Camping.* Mechanicsburg, PA: Stackpole Books, 2005.

Index

Note: Italicized page numbers indicate photographs or illustrations.

About the Authors

Mari Høe-Raitto is a native of Norway and has been competing in Nordic-style mushing since the age of fourteen. She raced successfully in Norway for six years and has been equally successful in her racing career—as both skijorer and sprint musher—since coming to the United States. Mari holds a bachelor's degree in physical education from the University of Alaska Fairbanks and is currently working on her M.Ed. in counseling at UAF. She is a certified Nordic ski instructor. She is recognized as an expert on skijoring in the United States and has appeared on radio and TV to promote the sport. Mari has written articles on dog driving for *Alaskan Gangline* and *Mushing* magazines. She owns and operates Raitto Kennels and Petcare, a boarding and training facility in Salcha, Alaska, for pets and working dogs. Mari has a son, Gard, and two daughters, Siri and Adeline.

Carol Kaynor holds a bachelor of arts in journalism/creative nonfiction from Vermont College and a master of fine arts in creative nonfiction from the University of Alaska Fairbanks. She has written articles on skijoring for *DogSport*, *Dog World*, and *Mushing* magazines, among others. Carol was a senior editor at

Mushing in 1987–1988 and skijoring editor in 1990. She moved to Fairbanks from New England in 1977 and learned to skijor during her first winter in Alaska. She is also a limited-class sprint musher and has been an active member of the Alaska Dog Mushers Association since 1985. Carol has had the privilege of owning several Alaskan huskies passed to her from other racing kennels because of their challenging personalities.

Carol and Mari founded the Alaska Skijoring and Pulk Association in 1987, and in the late 1980s they helped persuade the Alaska Dog Mushers Association to add skijoring to its regular race season. After several years of passionate lobbying for international recognition of skijoring as a legitimate sport, Carol was instrumental in pushing through the addition of a skijoring class to the International Federation of Sleddog Sports World Championships in 2001. Carol and Mari have copresented numerous clinics and lectures on skijoring.